COLLECTED WISDOM

of

Dr. Raymond Charles Barker

Hay House, Inc.

Carson, CA

Published and distributed in the United States by:

Hay House, Inc.
1154 E. Dominguez St.
P.O. Box 6204
Carson, California 90749-6204

The author of this book does not dispense medical advice or prescribe the use of any technique as a form of treatment for physical or medical problems without the advice of a physician, either directly or indirectly. The intent of the author is only to offer information of a general nature to help you in your quest for emotional well-being and good health. In the event you use any of the information in this book for yourself, which is your constitutional right, the author and the publisher assume no responsibility for your actions.

Library of Congress Cataloging-in-Publication Data

Barker, Raymond Charles.
Collected wisdom of Dr. Raymond Charles Barker.
p. cm.
ISBN 1-56170-097-5 (pbk. : alk. paper) : $10.95
1. United Church of Religious Science--Doctrines. I. Title.
BP605.U53B37 1994
299' .93--dc20 94-32867
CIP

ISBN 1-56170-097-5

98 97 96 95 94 5 4 3 2 1
First Printing, October 1994

Printed in the United States of America

The one mind created me as an individualization of itself. I am the mind of God in action, and this is right action. I am undisturbed by criticism, for I know who and what I am. I am poised and established in the mind of God, and nothing can disturb the calm peace of my soul. I accept this subconsciously, and so it is.

— Dr. Raymond Charles Barker

CONTENTS

FOREWORD

My own spiritual journey began many years ago at the First Church of Religious Science in New York City, where Dr. Raymond Charles Barker was the founder-minister. Dr. Barker's church was the place where I first heard that if I would change my thinking, I could change my life. I will always be grateful for this experience. Today, because of his help and teachings, I can now help others to change their lives.

I remember Dr. Barker as a brilliant teacher, clear in his thinking and in his speaking. He was always respected and loved. His humor made it easy to put his insightful points across. I, along with all of his students, will remember him with great love and affection.

I remember him saying to me when I first became a Practitioner: "Louise, remember, none will come to you but those that the Father has sent." Meaning that only people who I could help would come to me, and not to worry about being good enough.

It was at Dr. Barker's church that I began to explore my childhood beliefs, weeding out the negative ones. There, I learned to connect with the Power within me to shape and create a life I wanted to live. I learned the tools to change my own life for the better. Today, I am not at all like the scared, resentful, self-pitying person struggling for money who once entered Dr. Barker's church doors. Much that I am and have today I owe to his teachings.

I have come so far, and it is now my joy, pleasure, and privilege to present these unpublished writings to the public in book form. May Dr. Barker's wisdom and insights inspire us all for many years to come.

— Louise L. Hay,
author of *You Can Heal Your Life*

FOREWORD

Dr. Raymond Charles Barker. Just the mere sound of his name resonates with strength, with assurance, with all the qualities necessary to be a great leader. I speak of him, I think of him, with reverence and respect.

He was a giant in stature, both physically and spiritually. A giant of a teacher, a giant of an author, a minister, a human being.

I was fortunate enough to know him, not only on a colleague level, but on a social level. We had dinner together almost every Friday night for about 10 years. Dinner with Dr. Barker was like going to a seminar. How many people do you know who, while you're having dinner with them, are taking notes?

He knew the pillars of the New Thought Movement personally, and well. He knew the founders and many of the great teachers of Religious Science and Unity and Divine Science personally, and well. He certainly was a pillar himself, but he didn't like to be called that.

I was with Dr. Barker during his last days on this planet. His memorial service was held in my church with many of the great teachers and leaders of many churches attending and paying tribute to this great man.

I would like to think of this Foreword as being spelled "Forward," for this was and is the purpose of his writings — for us to move forward in our own personal lives and in this world. Dr. Barker wrote many wonderful books, articles, and pamphlets, but one of my favorite quotes of his, "Yesterday ended last night," has been a tremendous help when I get caught up in the past. In fact, that quote was on his last notes that he wrote for this world.

Dr. Barker said, "Work with your world the way it works. Life is a process of Intelligence. To drive a car, you have to drive it the way a car is driven. You don't drive it the way you would an airplane or a boat." Doesn't that make spiritual sense?

So, life can be lived according to the basic patterns of Life itself.

The most glorious thing about Dr. Barker's writings is that the ideas work, and they make sense. Dr. Barker wrote his books, gave his lectures, and lived his life with the desire that people would be helped and healed by what he wrote and what he said. I am fortunate to be one of those people.

Read his magnificent words, and think about them, and go forward in every area of your life.

— Dr. Tom Costa, author of
Life! You Wanna Make Something of It?
Palm Desert (California) Church of Religious Science

CHAPTER 1

WHAT IS RELIGIOUS SCIENCE?

Opening Remarks

I AM TALKING this morning about "What is Religious Science?" because the oldtimers need to be reminded, and the newcomer needs to be informed. Also, we need to know how to explain it to people who ask, "What is Religious Science?" "Why do we need another religion?" "If it isn't Christian Science, what is it?"

For our opening Treatment, I would like to build a mood. If there is one thing we believe more than anything else in Religious Science, we believe that we exist in God. Now, you may ask, "Doesn't everyone?" No, not as we do. We stress the fact that God is everywhere, evenly present, and that the totality of God is at every point in space and in every instant of time.

It is true we use a different vocabulary. We say that we exist in, and are a part of, one eternal Mind, Spirit, and Law. We are using 20th-century terms to explain the ageless creative process. We are saying it in a different language, but we are saying the same thing that the ancients said, that whatever the Creative Power is, It is where we are at every instant. It is in us at every instant. It is acting through us at every instant. It is a greater intelligence than our own. It is a greater emotion or love than our own. And, the full possibilities of this Creative Power, Mind, and Spirit are available to us upon our recognition of it. That sounds very complicated, but it isn't.

Twenty-five years ago I first heard Ernest Holmes, the founder of Religious Science, give a Sunday morning sermon in a vast theater to a large congregation. I sat there and listened, and I did not understand ten things the man said. I am sure this was equally true the first time I read the *Science of Mind* textbook. It made no sense to me. It did not register. Then after a while, it began to filter through my consciousness. I began to see what this larger concept was and my place in it. Gradually, as I studied and worked, the whole concept dawned on me. I exist and you exist in this Infinite Wisdom, Mind, Intelligence, which is perfect, complete, and sustained, and all of It is available to us.

The Treatment

LORD, Thou hast been our dwelling place in all generations. Before the mountains were brought forth, or ever thou hadst formed the earth and the world, even from everlasting to everlasting, thou art God (Psalm 90:1-2).

Therefore, right here and right now, here in Town Hall and in every home where they are listening by radio, we are in an Eternal Presence of pure wisdom, spirit, life, and love. We are immersed in it. It is flowing through us. We belong to It, and It belongs to us. There is One God, One Mind, One Spirit, One Truth, One Law of Its Action, One Eternal Good. And we know it. So be it.

The Sermon

Religious Science, as a teaching, began around 1926. By that time, Ernest Holmes had consolidated his thinking, his investigations, his study, and put it together into a single idea or volume called *The Science of Mind.* However, Religious Science could not have happened in 1926 had there not been an atmosphere that had been in the process of being produced for over 60 years. To get the true story of Religious Science, you have to go back to 1860.

I am not going to belabor you with history because those of you who know us well, know it. However, in 1860, a revolution took place in the spiritual thinking of the eastern United States. Following the great influence of the Unitarians and the Universalists, who had opened doors of the mind and rid them of many of the old theological doctrines, there appeared the concept of spiritual healing, a concept that had been left out of Christianity from about the time of A.D. 400. This was also the time of Emerson, who was widely read, who had opened many doors in people's minds.

People will say that there was spiritual healing down through the history of the Christian Church. Yes, but only in the form of non-understood miracles, usually produced by saintly characters or by people who were later announced to be saints. It certainly was not a doctrine for the general public. But, in 1860, through many illumined minds, there appeared the new concept that any person—whether in the church, out of the church, Catholic, Jewish, Protestant, Mohammed—could be healed through a mental science. This was new, and this was startling. It spread throughout the United States like wildfire.

This history of these early days is a fascinating story. For those of you who want it, there is one excellent reference book, *Spirits in Rebellion*, by Dr. Charles Braden. This history of these early days and what went on is the story of courageous men and women who stood up and said, "You do not need to be sick, limited, poor, afraid, and in desperate troubles. There is an action of the creative power of God in you and through you which you can call upon." Not an external God like the old theology, but the concept of an internal God. Our pioneers announced that the individual was designed by a Divine Intelligence to be a perfect person.

This was revolutionary. It isn't today. But, I can assure you that back in 1860, 1870, and 1890, the persecution on the part of the general public, the misunderstanding, the misinterpretation, and the ridicule was very great. Despite this, this new thought grew and grew, and by 1900 it was a well-established idea. Metaphysical churches of many kinds under many names had sprung up all over the United States. It was no longer just on the Eastern seaboard; it had gone across the country and was also penetrating the British Isles and other English-speaking areas. By 1900 there was a fertile field already sown. There were tremendous quantities of literature available. There were many magazines to be read, more magazines than we have today. In those days magazines were easier to produce, cheaper to produce, easier to distribute, and they were not taking the tremendous financial risks that you do in publishing a religious magazine today.

By 1900, we had the well-established field of Christian Science, the well-established beginning of the Unity movement. We had the Divine Science Church established. We had many other groups like these across the country. On a Sunday morning in the city of New York, you could have gone to one of twelve churches of this kind of thinking, this kind of believing: teaching the omnipresence of God as Mind and the perfection of the individual. These were the great key ideas that ran through it all.

So, when Ernest Holmes, one of five brothers born on a farm in Maine, moved to Boston, he became interested in Christian Science and studied it diligently. However, he did not join the church, nor was he active in the church. He was never a Christian Science Practitioner or teacher, but he was vitally interested and kept studying. One day in a Boston bookshop, he came across a copy of a book, *The Edinburgh Lectures*, by Thomas Troward, a series of lectures given in Edinburgh, Scotland, by this very scholastic, very brilliant, academic-minded man. This book changed Ernest Holmes' thinking. Finding it, he no longer studied Christian Science. Troward had given him the additional key that he needed, and he went to work bringing together a new system of mental and spiritual science.

He labored long at this time. He talked in New York and in other cities. However, he soon developed the

California bug that people get. He went there in 1916, and between 1917 and 1919 he lectured in the Grand Theater in Los Angeles. It was during this time that he was assimilating and writing the *Science of Mind* textbook. In 1920 he made trips east to lecture on the Science of Mind. When the textbook, *The Science of Mind*, was finally published, it caused no stir at all. No one was really interested. There were plenty of other books on the subject, not as Mr. Holmes discussed it and outlined it, but by better known and excellent teachers of that period. At that time he was not one of the well-known teachers. In Los Angeles, a few people became interested in him. He gave talks in people's homes, and soon he moved to a small theater in the Ambassador Hotel, giving talks on Sunday mornings at eleven. Within a short time, that was filled; it seated 400, and he moved to the Biltmore Hotel ballroom and overflowed it within a year. He moved on to larger halls until he rented the big Wiltern Theater on Wilshire Boulevard. Here, every Sunday morning for years he talked to 3,000 people. It was there that I first heard him in 1940.

In the meantime, Holmes had organized the teachings and was teaching classes. In those days, it was called the Institute of Religious Science. Mr. Holmes said, "I do not want to found a church. We have had enough churches. We don't need any more churches. We need class instruction. I want to produce teachers, not preachers. I do not need orators. I need people who can show other people how to change the patterns in their subconscious mind through a spiritual technique and thereby be liberated from their troubles."

For many years Mr. Holmes was the head of the Institute of Religious Science. With this, Religious Science began to spread. He published his magazine called *Science of Mind*. This is a well-known publication, now read around the world, having a very large circulation with a fine reading audience that appreciates it. With his magazine started, his textbook being sold, more books came out from the wisdom of Mr. Holmes. He was training Practitioners and teachers. In 1930 an Institute in Hollywood was developed by Dr. Robert H. Bitzer, then another Institute began in Glendale, California. Soon, branches were appearing all through California. I first affiliated myself with Ernest Holmes in 1945, and at that time, there were Religious Science Institutes all over California.

We were Institutes, not churches. But many of us who were teaching balked at the word *Institute* because people would ask, "Where do you go to church on Sunday?" The answer would be, "I go to the Institute!" "Oh! Why don't you go to a church?" In those early days, you will be interested to know that Ernest Holmes did exactly what I am doing here in New York City. The only music he had at his Sunday morning lectures was an organ. People were after him, saying that they ought to have more music. He would say, "Why? I thought you came to hear me. I have the theater full of people coming to hear what I have to say. Why do I have to put in anything more? They are coming to hear the messages." Later, he added a violin soloist, and finally he was persuaded to put in the hymns.

A few years ago, this church reverted to his original ideas. We have divested ourselves of that which is, to my way of thinking, unnecessary symbolism. The teachings continue to spread. In 1946, Mr. Holmes asked me to come to New York. At this time, there were no Churches of Religious Science east of the Rocky Mountains. He asked if I would go East. I was glad. I am one of those who have the Eastern bug, the way many people have the California or Texas bug. I was glad to come back, having been an Easterner, and you oldtimers know what has happened since then. We are celebrating the 20th anniversary of our Church. Out of our Church has come the entire field of Religious Science this side of the Mississippi. All came as the result of the work that you and I have done here in New York. With New York established as a prestige center, the other Churches throughout the South and Middle West developed. We people in New York, without any ego, can take credit for the Religious Science growth from the

Mississippi River to the Atlantic Ocean.

That is the outer history. You may ask, "Why did you change the name from Institute to Church?" We changed to Church because a number of ministers wanted to, and particularly here in New York I found a great resistance to the word *Institute* when used in conjunction with Sunday morning services. People didn't mind going on Tuesday night to a class at an Institute, but on Sunday morning at eleven o'clock, they wanted to go to a church. I was much younger, and I was proud of being a minister, and I wanted to be the minister of a Church, not an Institute. A number of us tried to persuade Mr. Holmes. He would never argue. He would always say, "Well, try it." When we went to him and said that we would like to change to *churches*, he answered, "I don't agree with you. I think you are wrong, but I don't know. So, try it. People, after a while, forget the name. If you are a good teacher, they will remember you and come to hear you. If you aren't a good teacher, it doesn't make any difference what name you have over the door."

One time in Los Angeles, Mr. Holmes announced that he had graduated a class of 200 Practitioners of Religious Science. I said, "Ernest, what on earth are you going to do with 200 Practitioners? You have hundreds now. The country is littered with Practitioners, and you can't train 200 Practitioners and train them well."

He said, "Barker, I'll tell you something. Train them, train them, train them, and those who aren't any good won't get any clients anyway. If I get 5 good Practitioners out of a class of 200, I am doing well. Don't worry about the 195; no one will ever go to see them about problems."

What is Religious Science? Mr. Holmes always liked to call it a study of the Thing Itself, what It does, and how to use It. He believed that the only logical synonyms for God were those of Mind, Spirit, Law, Love, and It. People used to shudder when Mr. Holmes would talk about "It." I know there are people in this Church who do not like it when I speak of God as It. I am not disrespectful. Whatever the Power is, It has to be impersonal. Whatever the Power is, whatever the Creative Intelligence is, It has to be impersonal. It cannot be personal and be what It is, and work the way we know It works. The Divine Mind is impersonal. Being impersonal, It must by Its own nature give of Itself to all. It can have no lines of distinction. There are no special gates of heaven for anyone. There is only an impersonal Givingness in which we are forever immersed and from which we draw according to our receptivity.

The opening four chapters of the *Science of Mind* textbook, the basic instruction of this Church, are named "The Thing Itself," "The Way It Works," "What It Does," and "How to Use It." If you want to, you can change one word: "What Is God?" "What Does God Do?" "How Does God

Work?" and "How Do You Use the Power of God?" Ernest Holmes stressed, from the beginning, the impersonal nature of the Divine Mind, the Divine Presence, the Divine Power. It is available to all, the religious and the nonreligious, those with no interest in spiritual thinking at all, as well as those who are deeply interested in it. The Power responds by corresponding. It becomes to us what we are to It. There are no copyrights on the kingdom of heaven, or on any other spiritual idea that may be around. This is the basis of Religious Science.

He stressed from the beginning, as had Mrs. Eddy and other teachers, that your application of It is the complete and important item in your experience. You may ignore It. You may use It as a hobby. You may use Religious Science as a place to go on Sunday morning. You may use It as you will. The Power doesn't care. But to reap the benefits of your knowledge of Mind, your knowledge of Science, you must actually take time to practice right thinking. You must practice the technique of Treatment which is the method by which we change the mind.

Do we believe in spiritual mind healing? We certainly do. But, please note that in Mr. Holmes' writings and in my writings we stress that it is a spiritual mind healing. We are not dealing with healing as it has been usually understood, such as the healing through the laying on of hands, and the other forms of healing used by orthodox churches. This is not our way of working. We are not saying our way of working is better. We are saying that it is the way it works for us. We respect what they are doing in other churches, and we know how they do it, but it is not our method. We use a totally non-emotional method of spiritual mind healing, non-emotional in the sense that we do not use anything to stimulate the senses in order to produce the healing.

We believe very definitely in spiritual mind healing. We practice it. The way we practice it is through a daily study routine that changes the consciousness of the individual. The essence of Religious Science is the change of your thought.

Religious Science is not trying to prove God. We are assuming that has been done. We are not trying to prove any savior, except that every man is his own savior. The illustrations in the Bible give us clues to our own individual capacity to save ourselves from the destructive actions of our own minds, which is the only salvation that is necessary.

Do we believe in Jesus? Yes, we believe in Jesus. Do we believe in the Old Testament? Yes. Do we believe in the Ten Commandments? Yes. Do we believe in the Sermon on the Mount? Yes. Do we believe in the Virgin birth? No. Do we believe in the Resurrection? No. Do we believe that we are all going to live happily together in heaven afterwards. No. We haven't lived happily here together, so why should we think we are going to do it somewhere else?!

I will sum this up in a very simple way. I will personalize this because it may help you. I am alive, but I didn't create myself. This which I am, while it appeared by means of my parents, was not created by them. Any woman who has ever had a child is fascinated with what goes on within her body in the nine months of pregnancy. Here is something being formed that she couldn't form. Here is something following a logical, scientific procedure according to medicine. Here is something being produced that the mother isn't producing. I believe in the miracle of every man's and every woman's birth. I know I am alive, but I didn't create life. I didn't create myself. With all the respect and affection that I have for my mother and father, here I am, different in many ways from my parents.

I have a mind that I can use two ways. I can use it destructively, because I have seen myself do it. I have seen myself in a rage. I know what it did, and I know what it did to me. I am not fooling myself one bit. I can use my mind in two ways. I can use it the other way, which I do more and more, for a creative, constructive purpose. What is this mind that I am using? I didn't create it. I didn't create it any more than I did life. I didn't create the mind that began to function in me shortly after birth. The brain was there, but mind began to function; consciousness began to function as awareness. I began to wake up to colors, to sounds, to people. I realized eventually that this woman who was taking care of me was special to me, and the man who came home at six o'clock and looked into the crib and said certain things in a certain kind of voice must be important to me, too. My mind was waking up.

I look around me at all the things that I have had through my life and all the experiences that I have had. I look at things and realize I couldn't create those, but someone's mind did. I didn't create this microphone into which I am speaking this morning, but someone's mind did. Where did they get the idea? They must have gotten it somewhere. I think of the things I have done, many of them new, many of them affecting the good of many people. Where did these ideas come from? So, I assure that I exist in an Eternal Presence. It is the Presence of a larger Mind, a larger emotion, a larger sense of everything, and It is always available to me. The way that I receive benefits is to think about It. So, I think about It, and as I think about It, the ideas of It happen in me. This is Religious Science.

Ernest Holmes had a very great mind. He said, "Someday something greater than Religious Science will come along." Of the book he had written, *The Science of Mind*, he said, "A better book will be written someday.

Truth is a continuity, and it will always unfold. It will always reveal Itself in new ways, in greater ways, perhaps in clearer ways."

You may ask: What about sin and salvation? What about heaven and hell? What about the day of judgment and the resurrection day? I don't know. These are theological theories that have garnered the respect of millions. I only know, like the wise have known, that I am, I think, I create, and yet that which I am, and that with which I think, and that with which I create is a Mind that is greater than myself. To me, this is Religious Science.

The Closing Treatment

"LORD, Thou hast been our dwelling place in all generations." This is the omnipresence of Spirit, Mind, and Love. "And let the beauty of the Lord, our God, be upon us and establish, Thou, the works of our hands unto us." We are immersed in and a part of the Eternal Presence, the One Mind, the One Spirit, and the One Truth. The beauty of It is upon us. And unto us is given the answer to our thought, the answer to our love, the answer to our idea. Amen.

CHAPTER 2

HEALING THROUGH CLEAR THINKING

"Now when he had ended all his sayings in the audience of the people, he entered into Capernaum.

"And a certain centurion's servant who was dear unto him, was sick, and ready to die.

"And when he heard of Jesus, he sent unto him the elders of the Jews, beseeching him that he would come and heal his servant.

"And when they came to Jesus, they besought him instantly, saying that he was worthy for whom he should do this.

"For he loveth our nation, and he hath built us a synagogue.

"Then Jesus went with them. And when he was now not far from the house, the centurion sent friends to him, saying unto him, Lord, trouble not thyself: for I am not worthy that thou shouldest enter under my roof:

"Wherefore neither thought I myself worthy to come unto thee: but say in a word, and my servant shall be healed.

"For I also am a man set under authority, having under me soldiers, and I say unto one, Go, and he goeth and to another, Come, and he cometh and to my servant, Do this, and he doeth it.

"When Jesus heard these things, he marvelled at him, and turned him about, and said unto the people that followed him, I say unto you, I have not found so great faith, no, not in Israel.

"And they that were sent, returning to the house found the servant whole that had been sick." (Luke 7:1–10)

IN THIS SCIENCE we talk a great deal about treatment, and newcomers are aware that treatment is quite different from the customary form of prayer. They are bewildered by it, yet they sense that there is something of value in it.

There is nothing miraculous about treatment. There is nothing mystic about it. There is nothing occult about it.

We use a Law of Mind the way you use any other law. We use the Law of Mind as casually as you use the law of electricity when you turn on a light. You use it simply and easily. We, in turn, use a Creative Law simply and easily.

We not only teach Spiritual Healing, we practice it. There are hundreds of people reading this book who could tell of their results from spiritual mind treatment. Our Movement started 90 years ago with the healing of Phineas P. Quimby, who, after he was healed, decided he would find out how he was healed. Isaac Newton was struck on the head by an apple and later discovered the Law of Gravity. Quimby was healed, and later discovered how he was healed. Charles and Myrtle Fillmore were healed, and when they discovered how they were healed, they set up the organization named Unity. Almost all of the modern healing movements are the result of their founders having had healings, and later discovering why they had them. Whether you have had an actual physical healing through this study or not, you now have a definite science to produce one. We know how to heal, because pioneer teachers investigated the Law of Mind and developed the technique of spiritual healing.

In the book, *Mind Remakes Your World*, there is the story of Henry Victor Morgan's healing. Henry Victor Morgan was the minister of the Divine Science Church in Tacoma, Washington, and all oldtimers in Truth knew him. He wrote on page 216:

"From the time I was twenty-one, and until I was thirty-seven, a condition for which the doctors knew no cure, had its hold on me." (It happened to be epilepsy). "In my hour of greatest darkness, when even hope was almost dead, a little pamphlet on spiritual healing was given me, which contained these words—'Man is in God's image and likeness, therefore the truth about God is the truth about spiritual man. This is the truth that Jesus said would set you free.'"

Then he added, "Something within me said, 'If this is so, I will never have another convulsion.' And nearly forty healthful and health-giving years have passed since then and I never have." On the next page he writes, "The news of my healing soon brought many to me seeking help. I then discovered a wonderful thing: that by simply holding people in mind, and thinking earnestly on the Power of God that healed me, marvelous cures were made."

Let us analyze what Morgan did. He read a statement of spiritual truth and said to himself, "I accept this. If this is so, I will never have another convulsion." And he never did. He was healed by his subconscious acceptance of a spiritual fact. Then, he found that by holding the name of any person in his mind, and thinking the same thought for him that he had thought for himself, the patient was cured. That is exactly what a Practitioner does when he treats a patient. The Practitioner holds the name of the patient in mind, and makes statements of Truth regarding the patient, and the patient is healed.

The patient is healed because we are all one in Mind at the subconscious level. We are individual and separate only at the conscious mind level. About 30 years ago, the great psychiatrist Carl Jung developed the theory that he named the Collective Unconscious. Anyone interested in his ideas can read his books (such as *Man and His Symbols*), which are among the finest in the field of psychiatry. Naturally, he did not believe what we believe, but he implies that at the subconscious level of life, we are one.

The subconscious mind has no time or space limitation. The conscious mind does. Your subconscious mind is not time or space conditioned; it is not personality conditioned. Most people think of their subconscious as their memory. That is one of the least important phases of the subconscious mind. At the subconscious level, you are one with everyone you have ever known, everyone you now know, and everyone you will ever know. At the subconscious level, because it is not a time- and space-conditioned element, what you know at one point in space can be known at another point in space.

Dr. J. B. Rhine of Duke University spent 30 years proving telepathy, and he proved it beyond a shadow of a doubt. After he had studied and verified hundreds of thousands of experiments to prove it, he said in an interview that he wondered whether he had discovered telepathy or not. He inferred that what the world called telepathy might not be telepathy at all. Telepathy is the passing of thought, idea, or image from one person's mind at one location to another person's mind at another location. It is a movement of thought through space. Dr. Rhine was suspicious that thought didn't travel through space. He was suspicious that what we call telepathy is one idea appearing simultaneously at two points in a subjective intelligence. He was saying that what is known at one point can be known at another point, not by sending a thought, but because it is the automatic action of the universal subconscious to do just that.

At the subconscious level of mind, you are thinking everywhere. At the conscious level of mind, you are only thinking where you are. Subconsciously, you are omnipresent. The Bible states that you are the image and likeness of God. If God is omnipresent, then you are omnipresent. At the subconscious level of mind, you are everywhere. You are in all and through all. You always have been, you are now, and you always will be. What you call birth, growth, maturity, old age, and death are conscious mind evaluations; they are never subconscious mind realizations.

The most pleasant part of death is that you do not know when you die. You are the only one who knows you are still living. Everyone else believes you are dead.

We are all one in a Universal Mind, in which thought does not move, but in which thought is known. In the *Science of Mind* textbook, Ernest Holmes emphasizes that healing is accomplished not by sending thought, but by knowing Truth. We do not send thought, we do not hold thoughts, we do know an idea. What we know in our subconscious about any person is known in his subconscious, and because it is known in his subconscious, it changes him and he is healed.

You can heal people at a distance. We call this absent treatment. Jesus was not at the bedside of the Centurion's servant. Jesus did not speak to the man. Jesus did not send a thought or hold a thought. Jesus knew that within the man was a perfect pattern of health. You can select a loved one anywhere on earth and prove the healing power of God through your oneness in Mind. Say to yourself: "I now declare this treatment for John Smith in Elgin, Illinois." Then proceed to make definite statements of Truth. "This man is the perfect expression of a perfect God," and statements similar to that. When you finish, say, "This treatment is now completed. It has been subjectively accepted by me; therefore, it has been subjectively accepted by John Smith. Amen." A few days later you will receive a letter saying that the man is better.

We are teaching a definite technique. We are not saying that if you sit down, become too comfortable, shut your eyes, get a little sleepy, and mutter a few affirmations, that you will heal your patient. There is a definite technique to this Science. We are not merely expecting that the thought we are thinking is going to cross the State of New York, the State of Ohio, etc., and will finally reach Elgin, where it will find the right house and the right man. That is the peculiar idea that most people have about spiritual healing. They think that if they say some sweet statements, these thoughts will fly through the air with the greatest of ease. We do not work that way in this Science.

God is everywhere, evenly present. The Creative Power is everywhere as a subconscious medium through which a fact is known but not sent. You are in It, and the person you want to heal is in It. What you know you are, is known where he is. Because you have spoken the person's name, the treatment becomes a fact at his subconscious mind level. When it becomes a fact there, the body is healed, the problem is solved, and the demonstration is made.

The patterns of the subconscious mind determine the experience of every person. There is not a pattern in your subconscious mind that cannot be changed if you want to change it. Many psychiatrists say it is impossible to change basic patterns after 50 years of age. I have seen people 80 and 90 years old respond to spiritual treatment, get out of their sick beds, and walk. The patterns regarding health in your subconscious mind determine your experience. Those patterns are very clear and very definite. You know what your present health is.

A person with chronic indigestion thinks in terms of it. Did you ever know anyone with chronic indigestion who did not think of food all the time? It colors their whole pattern of behavior. This condition can be cured by spiritual therapy if the patient himself, or a Practitioner on the case, knows that in the subconscious mind of John Smith there is no pattern of indigestion, but there is a pattern for the perfect acceptance, assimilation, and elimination of ideas. That is the mental equivalent for the digestive system. The Practitioner says, "I now declare for John Smith that in his subconscious mind there is no pattern of indigestion. There is no subjective resistance to food. There is no failure to assimilate and pass on the idea of life. He accepts life, assimilates its ideas, rejoices in its ideas, and eliminates everything unlike those ideas from his consciousness." That is the way you work the Law of Mind to produce a healing.

You are one with anyone for whom you may wish to pray in the universe. I think it is better for the beginner to not treat himself. I find Raymond Charles Barker is the hardest person in the world for Raymond Charles Barker to heal. I always have a Practitioner treat me. Take someone else and use this technique. Practice it and you will be amazed. You do not send thought, you do not hold thought, you know Truth. And what you know is known in the patient.

Jesus knew for the Centurion's servant that he was well, and he was well. The Centurion has said, "You operate mind, Jesus, like I run my army. I say 'Go' and the soldiers go. I say 'Come' and they come. I say 'Do this' and they do it." So, Jesus, standing some distance from the house, knew a truth, and what he knew, being a positive, was known in the patient where there was a negative, and because a spiritual positive will always destroy a material negative, the patient was healed. You too can do this.

Meditation

A perfect God could only project a perfect creation. As I am a part of this universe, I must be God's perfect expression. There is no place in me for imperfection to operate. My thought is cleansed, my conscience is clear. The Holy Spirit of Life, Love, and Wisdom saturates my subconscious mind, and my body expresses wholeness.

I am the person whom God created like unto Himself. His Life is my life. His Health is my health. His Vitality is my vitality. I live because God lives; I am health because God is health. I accept this, and it is the Truth of my being.

CHAPTER 3

YOU CANNOT DIE

"Let not your heart be troubled: ye believe in God, believe also in me.

"In my Father's house are many mansions: If it were not so, I would have told you. I go to prepare a place for you.

"And if I go and prepare a place for you, I will come again, and receive you unto myself; that where I am, there ye may be also.

"And whither I go ye know, and the way ye know.

"I am the way, the truth, and the life: no man cometh unto the Father, but by me."

(John 14:1–6)

RELIGIOUS SCIENCE is a religion of life, a philosophy that negates the possibility of death. We believe that the universe is a living system—that life is in all, through all, and in action by means of all. We believe that every person who has ever been alive is still alive, and that we who are alive will always be alive, because we are in an unending life process called God. We believe in an eternal evolutionary plan called a cosmos—level after level, plane after plane, in which all people must by their very nature move forward.

Jesus talked about life and little about death. Jesus evidently realized that the consistent affirmation of the Life Idea was essential to his consciousness. Repeatedly, he told people that he would forever continue to be himself, and he told these same people that they would forever continue to be themselves.

If there is eternal life, then we have always lived. The very words "eternal life" mean forever. They must mean since time and space began, since the original Creative Action in the Universal Mind began to know Itself as man. You have always been alive. And, you have always been alive just as you are now. You are going to ask, "Why can't I remember this eternal existence?" Rejoice that the Infinite Intelligence, the Divine Order, is such that you cannot remember everything. You do not remember many unpleasant things that happened ten years ago. Why should you want to remember untold millions of years? It is good that we have a divine "forgettory," as well as a divine memory.

Eternal life is the movement of consciousness in the Mind of God. No one knows when this started. We only know that it could not have had a beginning; it must have always been, and it must forever be. The Universal Presence is a Creative Presence because It is forever making things out of Itself. The first chapter of Genesis states that the entire cosmic order is the result of an action in God whereby creation was produced in God, and we are in the permanent Presence and can never be out of It. God said, "Let there be," and there was.

The Infinite Presence is alive. Its nature is activity under intelligence operating by means of law. The Universal Presence which is God, is Spirit or Intelligence. It acts through Law and Order and always produces that which is beneficent. The cosmic order is a beneficent system. You may not see it that way, but it is. When you are happy, you think that the whole world is yours to use. You recognize it for what it really is.

The Creative Process is spiritual. It is God in action, producing out of Himself, and all things are forever alive in Mind. Physics have discovered that the universe is a living system, that there is no inert matter. The universe is alive. As the physicists break down matter into lesser parts, they are breaking down temporary forms of motion, temporary forms of energy, which are pulsating with Intelligence according to law. Every atom in this paper booklet is complete within itself. It is a separate, vibrating, alive entity in the universe, and it is motion. The page you are reading is a force, an energy, a power, a light—it is not merely paper. Every cell of your body is alive; every atom of the walls around you is alive—there isn't anything dead. And if there isn't anything dead, then there is no death.

You are liable to think that all this is a very good argument, but one day you will be 99 years old, and you will die. No, you won't. You will merely change bodies, which is a healthy, normal thing to do. You have been doing that all your life; there is nothing new to that. You have been changing your body every year since the instant you were conceived. The body that emerged from your mother's womb only remained that size for a very short time. Within a matter of months, you had a whole new body. The baby's body changes completely in nine months. The adult's body takes longer to change. You have been wearing one body after another. You have been wearing more bodies than you have lived years, because your body is always changing. It is forever changing because there is a Divine Plan that is changing it. There is a Power that acts and that knows exactly what It is doing.

We call it God, Spirit, and Mind. There is a Divine Design in the midst of a living universe causing a constant change, a constant movement, and a constant flow of activity through form.

The reason that I am certain I shall always exist is because I am certain of what I am now. The consciousness that I am now cannot be destroyed. If you ask yourself what you are, there is only one logical answer, either from the field of religion or the field of philosophy—you are consciousness. Consciousness is in body, and body is in consciousness—but the thing that you really are is consciousness. You change bodies every few months, but one consciousness goes through them all. If you are consciousness in a permanently changing body, then you, as consciousness, will always be, whether body is or is not. You may go to sleep tonight and use a different body in your dreams than the one that is lying dormant on the bed. The body in the dream is just as real as the one on the bed. It is a similar body, because body is the projection of consciousness, and as long as you have a body concept in your thought, you will always have a body in your world. This is why you need not worry about life after death, because you will always be in a world that you project, and you will always be using a body that you project.

Jesus said to the people in his day: "You are dependent upon me because you have made yourself dependent upon me. You think that I am necessary to you, so therefore I am necessary to you. I am going away, and where I am going you may come, and you will come because there is a law of evolution that will make you come. There are all kinds of places, there are all kinds of levels of life, because 'In my Father's house are many mansions.'"

As an illustration, we will use two television programs. You are watching Channel 4, and at the end of the program you decide to try Channel 2. When you change programs from 4 to 2, you change wavelengths, as each channel operates on its own wavelength. While you are listening to Channel 2, you are in that world; when you turn to 4, you are in *that* world. You have changed from world to world, by moving from one wavelength to another. When the time comes for you to leave your present body, you will move out of a wavelength called the present world into another wavelength where there is also a world, because this universe has worlds without end. All existence is vibration; all things are energy locked up temporarily as form. Everything is movement and flow, and this present world is actually nothing but a band of waves of energy. The universe is nothing but many wavelengths of energy, locked into form under Divine Intelligence. The Universe is nothing but many wavelengths of energy, which have within them a self-knowing Mind and an eternal togetherness of Love. This present world is only one band out of the entire scale of wavelengths.

The extrasensory perception authorities say that all of your senses could be extended. You do not see everything there is to be seen. Your cat sees more than you do. You may have a dog who sees more than you do. The visual area of the human eye is definitely a limited area. There are lights, colors, tones, and shades of color that you do not see. You are not seeing all of your world, even with normal optical vision. The same thing is true of all of the five senses. If you have normal hearing, there are still tones you do not hear. If you have a normal sense of taste, there are delicate flavors you do not taste. There are fragrances you cannot smell with the nose. All these are right here; you need not go to a place called heaven with beautiful flowers and unusually good food to extend your senses. All of the human senses have a possibility for extension.

When you die, it is similar to moving from Channel 2 to Channel 4, moving from one level or vibration to another, from one wavelength to another wavelength. That is all you do, and that is all anyone has ever done. Every teacher who ever taught is still teaching. Every artist who has ever painted is still painting, because life is a continuity. You are going to be forever you, moving from wavelength to wavelength, from level to level, or, as Paul would say, "From glory to glory even as by the Spirit of the Lord" (II Cor. 3:18). All this will be conscious. When you move from Channel 2 to Channel 4, you are immediately in the picture and the sound of Channel 4. Yet, everyone else looks at Channel 2, and the sorrow begins. While you are in Channel 4, enjoying it thoroughly, everyone else is at Channel 2, weeping. That is all that death is, because the Life of God cannot stop. You move from Channel 2 to Channel 4. There you have all life, intelligence, action, and consciousness. At the other channel they are declaring death. At Channel 4 you do not even know that you have died. "In my Father's house are many mansions." there are many levels, and on every level God is, Intelligence is, Love is, and people are, and we move from "Glory to Glory."

Meditation

The Life of God is the life of man. The life within me is spiritually perfect now and forevermore. God is on my pathway, and the future is alive with unceasing activity. I am not the victim of age and death; I am the unending life and love of God.

I think with Spirit and act with Law and Order. My world is my thought outpictured, and I am a permanent thinker in God's Mind. I am now, and I shall forever be. I move from glory to glory with ease, with progressed ideas and with a deeper sense of Truth. I rejoice in life, for God is within me, and increased appreciation of life is mine.

Chapter 4

No one stops you but yourself

"And he took his staff in his hand, and chose him five smooth stones out of the brook, and put them in a shepherd's bag which he had, even in a scrip; and his sling was in his hand; and he drew near to the Philistine.

"And the Philistine came on and drew near unto David; and the man that bare the shield went before him.

"And when the Philistine looked about, and saw David, he disdained him: for he was but a youth, and ruddy, and of fair countenance.

"And the Philistine said unto David, Am I a dog, that thou comest to me with staves? And the Philistine cursed David by his Gods.

"And the Philistine said to David, Come to me, and I will give thy flesh unto the fowls of the air, and to the beasts of the field.

"Then said David to the Philistine, Thou comest to me with a sword, and with a spear, and with a shield: but I come to thee in the names of the Lord of hosts, the God of the armies of Israel, whom thou has defied.

"This day will the Lord deliver thee into mine hand: and I will smite thee, and take thine head from thee; and I will give the carcasses of the host of the Philistines this day unto the fowls of the air, and to the wild beasts of the earth; that all the earth may know that there is a God in Israel." (I Samuel 17:40–46)

"And it came to pass, when the Philistine arose, and came and drew nigh to meet David, that David hasted, and ran toward the army to meet the Philistine.

"And David put his hand in his bag, and took thence a stone, and slang it, and smote the Philistines in his forehead; that the stone sunk into his forehead; and he fell upon his face to the earth.

"So David prevailed over the Philistine with a sling and with a stone, and smote the Philistine, and slew him; but there was no sword in the hand of David." (I Samuel 17:48–50)

MODERN BIBLE scholars tell us that David probably did not kill Goliath, that great events are ascribed to great people in their time. It is still a magnificent story of the way the human mind works. Every problem you face is a Philistine who is armed against you, a negative that you have made of your own belief. Some day, sit back and watch what your mind does with a problem. When the problem appears, it startles you and you begin to fear it. Then, your imagination goes to work on what might happen if you did not solve it. The problems begin at the level of the minor, and you magnify it with your imagination and make it a major one. You make it a giant.

Whether there were giants in the days of David, I do not know. I suspect that David was short and the other man was tall, and they wrote it up years afterwards and made it dramatic. Whether David did slay the giant or not is unimportant. What is important is that I make giants out of my problems. If I didn't let my imagination work on them negatively, they probably would remain at a minor level and I could solve them.

Think of the ways in which your serious problems have a firm grip on your thinking. Then, your emotions rise to meet them, and your subconscious accepts them. When your imagination negatively goes to work, very shortly you have lost control. The problem now has you. Many people walk the streets of New York with a problem running them. Walking down Fifth Avenue, they do not see the beauty; they are too busy thinking about their problems. Many a dinner party has been ruined by one or two people who couldn't leave their problems outside the house. They may not mention their problems, but by their negative intensity and their seeming absentmindedness, you know something is wrong. The party didn't quite go over, because these problems controlled people who were no able to enter into the spirit of it.

I wish that we had a checkroom outside this Church, and everyone coming in here on Sunday morning in some unique way could leave their problems outside. While you were in the Church, you could then give your full attention to Spiritual Ideas. Many of us bring problems with us. Yet, in this Church at this instant there isn't a problem. You are comfortable and relaxed; everyone is all right. At this instant in your world, there isn't a problem unless it is in your mind, unless you brought it with you and continue to entertain it. You may revive it later when you leave. It may be at the office when you go there tomorrow morning. But, at this instant there isn't a problem.

In the midst of all your problems, you can pause in your thoughts, and say, "At this split second I do not have a problem." Our emotions put their tentacles around a problem and hang on to it. There is that in us which magnifies evil out of all proportion. The finest psychologists imply in their lectures and books that their therapy is to have the person with the problem gradually see the predicament at the level where it really is, and no longer distort it and magnify it by emotion.

You have nothing to deal with but yourself. When a problem stops you, it is due to emotional states that you have unconsciously allowed to stop you. Every teaching of the Bible is to have the individual solve his problem and live in a better world. The Bible does not teach the modern psychological therapy. The Bible offers a spiritual instruction. However, as it can only operate through the mind of the person accepting it, it becomes a psychological technique. That is why a religion that is not coupled with psychology is of little value to anyone. Religion states the nature of God and explains the action of God through the individual. Psychologically, your mind is the only place you experience anything. It is the only place where you experience life. Therefore, if religion is to be applied, it has to be applied through a mental science. We teach spiritual basis plus a thinking technique; therefore, we have a spiritual science.

The recognition that no one stops you but yourself, that you are your only enemy, and that you are your only problem, is not enough unless with it you have a technique enabling you to do something about it. David not only went toward Goliath, but he had a means of destroying Goliath. You can move toward the solution of your problem, provided you know that you have the means of overcoming your problem. The means of solving your problem is the right use of your present mental equipment.

When you discuss your problem, you tell people that there is nothing wrong with you that more money wouldn't cure, or more health, or a happy marriage, or some other thing that you mention. You still are not using the technique that Jesus taught, which was to not manipulate things, situations, conditions, or people, but to manipulate mind and emotion. Jesus was only doing one thing: he was changing thought. He knew that changed thought produced changed conditions. Most people have the cart before the horse. They rearrange their lives. The person who joyously moves into a new apartment and still takes his old self in, will find that soon the new apartment looks like the former one. The generating center in him didn't change when he left one street to move to another.

Think of your limitations once in a while, and ask yourself why they are limitations. You have accepted them as such. In your acceptance of them, you failed to realize that within you is a Power, an Intelligence, a Spiritual Know-How, which when recognized by you and employed by you through the tools of right thinking and right feeling, causes the problems to become nothing. When the limitation is accepted and the mental tools are not put into action, then you "wallow" in your problems and say, "Won't someone help me?"

There are plenty of people to help you. The only difficultly with someone else helping you is that you get out of your problems through his state of consciousness and not your own. Inevitably, you soon have a similar problem because *you* haven't grown out; someone else pulled you out. How many people have you loaned money to, and it has not helped them a bit? It met an emergency, yes. But, didn't they shortly have another one? I think it takes a greater wisdom to help people than most of us have. It takes wisdom to know when we are helping, and when we are merely continuing their problem. Of course, there are times that we can help.

When I am in a problem, if another lifts me out of it, have I grown on the inside by the experience? I doubt it. But, I can counsel within myself and say, "I am my own problem. I have accepted it. This problem has arisen in me. It is around me, and I am in it. I do not blame anyone for it. I do not blame any thing for it. I face the fact that I have it. What am I going to do about it?

Two things you do—you think and you feel. Over a period of time, you can develop a positiveness, a vision and a knowingness. Or, you can develop negatively, pessimistically, and gloomily. You can do either one. Realize that your mind is the center of the world, and that your thinking determines your experience. When you are clear on that, then work on yourself when you have a problem, instead of working on the problem. It is interesting how the problem disappears.

David slew Goliath. David represents that young quality of meeting problems. It is only young because you haven't used it enough for it to grow old. It is like the good china that you keep for special occasions. I learned years ago that anything good enough for my guests was good enough for me. Anything I use on a formal occasion, I use on any occasion when I am all alone, because the people I invite into my home are no better than I am.

No one stops you but yourself. The only enemy you have is yourself. The Philistines are of your own creation; they are the negatives that you have enlarged and allowed to grow until they appear terrific. Within you is a youthful Something, a spirit that is never aged, tired, dissipated, or unhappy. God in you says you do not need elaborate armor to destroy Goliath. You do not need swords; you need only do a very simple thing: Think straight, feel right, and believe that God doesn't want you to have the problem. Believe that the Presence of God within you solves the problem. That is the slingshot; that is the five stones.

Within you is an unconquerable Mind which, as you see your problem and deflate it, acts through your positive thinking under a Law, and the problem is met. It is met on time and in order. It is met without harm or hurt to anyone else. It is met because it is normal for Life to meet problems, when Life finds a soul that will be positive enough to let It do it.

CHAPTER 5

RELIGION AND YOUR HEALTH

Treatment for Health

GOD IS the life of man; therefore, God is my life now. This Life is governed, controlled, and expressed by Divine Intelligence. Every part and function of my body is the full action of Intelligent Life. Disease is ignorance; Health is the Mind of God in action.

I now subconsciously accept my life as Divine, Perfect, and Whole. No illness can operate in me; no bacteria can control me. My body is subject to God and to God alone. I now destroy through this treatment, which is the Word of Truth, all subconscious causes of disease. They no longer exist, and their results in my flesh are now erased for all time.

I affirm my health as permanent Divine Action, and I cooperate with the Divine Spirit indwelling me in all ways. I am spiritually guided to right eating, right relaxation, and right recreation. I rejoice in health and thank God for it. Amen.

TWENTY-FIVE YEARS AGO, this talk would have been a highly controversial subject. In the last 25 years, a tremendous change has taken place in public opinion. Now, the public perceives that metaphysics is respectable and demonstrable. Also, the fact that the mind affects the body is a generally accepted principle. Twenty-five years ago, we were considered "crackpots" in the religious field. Today, people come to us because the orthodox churches do not teach Spiritual Mind Healing, and these people want to know more about it.

I do not need to prove that your mind causes your body to be ill. You know that. Everywhere is the fad of psychosomatic medicine. Everyone seems to know a great deal about it, and accepts it, except when it applies to them personally. Like all psychological investigation, we always seek it for another member of our family. We investigate psychology to see when the other person is not reacting to life the way we think he should. Psychosomatics has become a part of the proven medical and psychological therapies. No longer do medical authorities tell us that all diseases arise from bacteria. They realize that at least a portion of disease does not.

In the field of psychosomatic medicine, the specialists have located mental and emotional origins for some diseases. Even the most enthusiastic psychosomatic doctors are very careful to say that not all diseases are of mental and emotional origin. We metaphysicians know that every single type of physical ailment originates from disturbed and incorrect emotional patterns in the subconscious mind. That is the teaching of Religious Science; that is what we believe, and that is what we demonstrate.

What does all this have to do with religion? You may ask, "Why doesn't Religious Science stay out of the field of health? You have such a wonderful philosophy. You have helped many people. You are giving a much more intelligent understanding of the relationship of man to his universe, his relationship to the Creative Power. Isn't that enough?"

Our teaching is of no value whatsoever if you can't prove it. One of the problems that orthodox churches have is that people accepted what they said because they did not have to prove anything. This is an instruction in which we do not say *believe*, we say *use* it. We do not even say *accept* it, we say *prove* it. If you have been in Religious

Science for a number of years and are as sick as you were before, you might as well have attended other churches. If, in Religious Science at the end of five years, you are not better off financially than you were before, you should find another teaching. Our whole premise is that an enlarged and correct understanding of the nature and operation of Mind will produce improvements in your world. It should make your health greater. It should make your financial world easier. It should make your whole area of life better.

Until the time of the Golden Age of Greece, medicine and the priesthood were one. In all the oldest religions, the priest was also the doctor. It was not until the time of the Greeks that religion and medicine went two varying ways, developing a church, a priesthood, and an ecclesiastical authority that no longer filled the needs of the physical problems of it followers. Then, the beginnings of the medical profession developed, and gradually it has become a science. That split was probably a necessary one. It certainly has lifted medicine out of the field of the mysterious, the weird, and the occult. At the same time, we, as human beings have suffered because we divorced bodily health from religious principles. The church has been solely interested in the soul of man, in his living this life on a moral basis, and in equipping him for a life hereafter. The medical field, without any religious background, has taken care of the physical body during man's sojourn on this planet.

Religious Science is gradually bringing these two approaches together. Many of the clergy are talking in psychological terms rather than in theological terms. Great masses of people are beginning to see that a psychological therapy without a spiritual premise is not a permanent healing technique. There is interest in a concept of life that does not make psychology ridiculous by teaching about a god on a throne. Out of this interest has emerged this present religious group who has seen that whatever the nature of Life is in the individual, It is of a spiritual origin, meaning that it is not self-originated.

You are alive out of an Aliveness of God. You are That which causes life to be. You have free will. You can direct this life any way you wish—good, bad, or indifferent. Nevertheless, that quality of life which is Life is neither man originated, man maintained, nor man explained. It can only be understood as a universal Creative Power, which as it individualizes Itself, creates out of Itself the individual. Therefore, the life which you are is the One Life individualized as you. As It is the one life individualized as you, It is empowered to act according to your decision. Life has the qualities of intelligence, of order, and of production. You are alive, but this Life which you are living indicates by what It does for you that It has intelligence. It knows what to do. It has order because it always creates through order. That which you call disorder is merely order appearing in a way you do not like it. Disorder is a negative idea coming to the surface in an orderly way.

The Bible teaches healing through a spiritual, psychological technique or process. In both the old and the new Testaments is the teaching that as the sins of a person are released, health automatically appears. When your deep inner fears, your deep inner hurts, your deep inner concerns are brought to the surface and are denied, your health immediately improves. That statement is psychologically correct and is spiritually correct. The older churches have been forgiving the sins of man, but they have never related the sins of man to the causes of bodily disease. Bodily disease is not created by the kinds of sins that they have forgiven. The deep problems in the individual have not been released, exposed, and clarified by the usual theological systems. The basic causes of disease are not usually moral causes. Therefore, we need a new system of freeing the individual from these inner terrors. Within yourself, with or without the aid of professional help, you can change the basic pattern structure of your subconscious mind, and with that change you can have health. You can do it alone or with the aid of a professional Practitioner, a psychologist, a clergyman (if he knows how to do it), or a psychiatrist. When the subconscious emotional patterns are changed through a spiritual technique, the individual is healed quickly and permanently. A lengthy therapy is not involved.

There is a difference between the healing power of God and the healing power of psychological techniques. When a person is healed through a spiritual therapy, they are healed on the premise that within their mind is a center of pure Intelligence, a center of pure Life, which being the nature of God, knows what to do. It destroys the old pattern and creates the new. A psychological healing is premised upon the fact that you have only a human mind, and that there is no spiritual power in it. Through a technique of release, an old pattern comes to the surface and you see it for what it is. You then arrive at another human mind conclusion, and are therefore benefited in health. Both work. But, Religious Science is teaching a spiritual therapy. The reason the individual mind can be clarified is because it has a Plus Element in it that is a spiritual quality. You are not a human mind; you are an individual using a Divine Mind humanly. There is the whole difference.

As you recognize your own mental and emotional processes as precursors to the formation of your world, you start the process of healing your own problems. Never start with an analysis of the problem. An analysis of the problem merely reaffirms the problem in your own mind. The healing begins when you know that within you Spirit is unconditioned and not sick, even though Life acts through a process that appears to be sick. When you went to bed last night, you were very tired. This morning after your second cup of coffee, you felt fine. The reason that you could feel fine this morning is because there is within you that which makes you well. The "you" that was tired and the "you" that woke up feeling rested is the same you. When you shut off the conscious mind for eight hours, Life knows exactly what to do to give you the refreshment that you need.

In the individual there is that which heals; there is that which responds to a positive spiritual healing technique. It does heal the body. It does heal emotional problems, and it does heal people of great fear. Your religion can heal you. Try it.

CHAPTER 6

GOD IN YOUR SUBCONSCIOUS

YOU MAY WONDER why a clergyman should talk about the subconscious mind. You might expect him to discuss the beauties of nature, or man's inhumanity to man, but why does he discuss the subconscious?

One of the reasons that the metaphysical movement has appeared and spread through the world is that between 1880 and 1900 there arose a new concept of man. The new concept of man required a new religious philosophy. It required a new instruction, a new technique, a new language. All this, orthodox theologies could not supply.

The subconscious mind was discovered by Anton Franz Mesmer and was explained by Freud. It is the basis of all forms of psychotherapy. It revealed the fact that man was predominantly a mental and emotional process and not merely a body creature. With man as the operation of mind, rather than man as only a body operation, you need a new understanding of what the Spirit in man is.

All former religious systems were premised upon the fact that man was a body. They demanded physical ways to maintain a healthy individual. Morality was based on what man did or did not do with his body. A man was considered virtuous if he did not drink, smoke, or commit adultery. Orthodoxy implied that man's body was his source of trouble. In the Old Testament, the laws of the Hebrews are laws dealing with body, food, sex, marriage, etc. In the New Testament, Paul took the idea of Jesus and translated them into a "body" teaching. Throughout the history of the church, we have been told about sin—don't do something with your body.

Jesus, 2,000 years ahead of his time, discovered and tried to say that man was not body; man was mind. Simple people heard him proclaim a great message. In the Four Gospels, you read his talks about belief and faith, about the positive, the constructive, and the creative.

Today, everyone is aware that the mind controls the body. Consciousness determines body. Jesus said that the body was something you could pick up and lay down, but that of itself it had no power. Your body does not make you do anything wrong. You decide something, and your body proceeds to do what you decide. Your body does not cause you to commit errors. You must want to commit them to have your body do them. Man's ways of thinking and feeling are his primary problem. Religious Science adapts its spiritual principles to an explanation and help at the point where you need help, which is in the mind.

The subconscious mind is the principal operation of your life. You are 90 percent subjective or subconscious. Everything you do, you do because your subconscious mind does the work. The area of the conscious and the subconscious and the interaction of the two is the whole cause and continuity of life. What you decide with the conscious mind, you produce with the subconscious mind. When you do not decide an issue with the conscious mind, then your subconscious mind takes the best material it has remaining from previous decisions and produces after its own kind.

If you fail to direct your subconscious mind, then it will produce under a law of averages, and you will be a nice, ineffective, sweet person. There are millions of such people. You ride with them on subways; you see them in your neighborhood—people who are neither good nor bad; they are merely average. They don't do anything evil for they have been told they would go to hell if they did. They aren't too good because that is an effort. They aren't bad enough to be in hell, and they aren't good enough to be in heaven. In Religious Science we have no heaven or hell, so there is no place for such people.

The important factor in your life is never what you are thinking at the instant; it is the sum total of all that you have ever thought. What you are thinking at the instant moves from the conscious mind into the subconscious mind automatically, and adds to the sum total. Unless your conscious mind is spiritually activated, it cannot do anything in the subconscious but merely add to its sum total. A spiritual concept or idea deliberately accepted by the conscious mind becomes a law of action at the subconscious level. There is a difference between a spiritual idea and an average idea. Average thinking is not a decisive direction to the subconscious, but spiritual thinking is a command to the subconscious to produce a good.

Each time you deliberately think in spiritual terms, your thought becomes a law of creative action. From primitive man to the present, people have prayed. They have prayed without knowing they had a conscious or a subconscious mind. It did not matter to them because they did not know whether they had one. As they prayed, they began to feel better. The more they prayed, the more that good appeared in their lives. Past generations developed a great belief in, and use of, prayer. They depended upon it to get them out of trouble.

Today, we have a different understanding of prayer, which we call the science of prayer. We know that prayer is a deliberate conscious mind selection of a spiritual idea, which then automatically becomes a Law of Mind action in the subconscious.

All life seems to be made up of two factors. In the past we have had the teaching of duality and of plurality. It was said that you could not know light unless you knew darkness because there would be no contrast. Many schools of philosophy believed that you had to know evil in order to consciously determine good. If all life is a dual action, then this dual action in the individual is the interaction of the conscious and subconscious mind. What has been known in the past as the individual's soul is his subconscious mind; and what was known in the past as the "Spirit in man" is his conscious mind.

The bibles, the prophets, the messiahs, and the saints have told us that when the Spirit enters into the soul of man, that he is thereby redeemed out of all nations, all creeds, and all problems. In other words, when your conscious mind deliberately accepts a creative idea and delivers it to the subconscious with a sense of authority, then the Law of the subconscious proceeds to produce in your experience what this idea has ordered done.

I repeat this for emphasis. You have heard in many orthodox sermons that when the Spirit of the Lord enters into the soul of man, that this man is redeemed out of his problem. In the terminology of Religious Science, we say that when the conscious mind of the individual deliberately selects a creative idea and delivers that creative idea to the subconscious mind, that the subconscious mind acts as a law and proceeds to produce the equivalent of that idea in the individual's experience. That is the whole teaching of Religious Science. Past generations called this process *prayer;* we call it *treatment*. Either word is good; I happen to prefer the latter. To me, the word *treatment* indicated an action of mind. It indicated a definite action taking place. It takes prayer out of the nebulous, and brings it into the factual.

When you have an omnipresent God, there isn't anyone to pray to, because It is everywhere. No more heaven, no more clouds; God is everywhere, and because It is everywhere, to most people It almost means that It is nowhere. Many people are uncomfortable in Religious Science because they would like to have a man in a gold chair. This would be more definite. If I could say that there is more God here where I am standing than there is where you are sitting, then you would focus your attention here with greater intensity. There is no more of God here than there is in the chair where you are seated. There is no more of God on this platform than there is on the street. God, being everywhere, the Creative Power of life being everywhere, It is never accentuated at any one point more than at any other. Being everywhere, It must be in me, and It must be in you. The universe gives evidence of an Intelligence that knows what to do and proceeds to do it. We can assume that the nature of God must be that of an Infinite Creative Mind, an Infinite Field of Creative Ideas, and that we are in It in order that each one of us shall be an inlet and an outlet of It.

This Creative Power works in your world automatically. The seed becomes the root, then the stem, and then the flower. But, in the individual, God does not act automatically. In the individual, there is that quality called will. The individual has the capacity of determination. Many a person states that he has free will, and then adds, "But, I can't lose weight." Anyone can lose weight who will drink water and have one toothpick a day. The person who says he cannot lose weight is the person who cannot make up his mind to do it. But he *can* do it.

The same thing is true of the person who says, "I can't change my job." What he means is that he subconsciously does not want to do so. The person who says, "I can't change my environment," has arrived at a point where he does not want to make the effort to do it. But, he can do it. There isn't a thing you cannot do if you want to do it. You have free will. People in this congregation have proven that they can get well through spiritual therapy, and have done it. Others in the congregation say they cannot get well. It depends entirely on the individual. You are the only thinker in your mind. You have the right to select any idea, and your subconscious mind will work out the idea that you have selected. The universe around you will reshape itself and reform itself for the accommodation of the new experience.

Jesus not only had the ability to prove the Creative Process for himself, he had the ability to do it for others. Jesus was a Practitioner in the finest sense of the word. He could subconsciously accept an idea, and the idea demonstrated itself. He did it constantly for himself and for other people.

Your subconscious mind is the producer of your experience. Your conscious mind is the deciding factor of your experience. Both of these are spiritual processes working together. They are the God Process in the individual, and by your use of them, you determine your life.

You can awaken from a mental and emotional lethargy and become a person in your own right. Or, you can remain in lethargy, be loved, be appreciated, and later be mourned. Life says to you that you can become what you choose only when you choose it and are willing to go through the necessary work to be it. That you can do, and I have faith that that's exactly what you are going to do.

Chapter 7

God does heal

SPIRITUAL HEALING is a controversial issue, and I like to discuss controversial issues. I believe in spiritual mind healing as definitely as I know I am standing on this platform in Town Hall this morning. I believe in it because I have seen it take place. I have seen it happen in my own body. I have known hundreds, if not thousands, who have been healed.

It intrigues me that not once in the last 25 years during which I have been an exponent of spiritual healing and a Practitioner of it has there ever been a single survey made by any responsible group of people as to the efficacy of mental healing. Never once has it been investigated. Yet, for 90 years this form of healing has been practiced obviously, publicly, and coast to coast in the United States of America. As a result of the work accomplished in this country, mental healing has encircled the earth. It is now practiced in every country in the world where there is liberalism in spiritual thinking.

Any time you study the beginning of any religious system, you discover healing. Behind every major denomination, the originator, or the originating group, practiced healing. As late as the Middle Ages, healing was, to a very great extent, in the hands of the clergy and not in the hands of medical doctors. Later when the cleavage came, healing moved from the church to the physician. From that time on, there have been two separate areas of life. When people are in need of peace of mind, they go to church. When they are in need of physical health, they go to their medical doctor. That has been the pathway from the Middle Ages to the present.

We appreciate the great developments in the field of medical research, giving us a great body of evidence that the physician does a good job. The public, however, supports the belief that any form of healing belongs in the standard medical field. But it doesn't.

The outsider says, "Are the healings that take place in Religious Science factual healings or are they merely neurotic conditions overcome?" They are factual healings. It is undoubtedly true that we have neurotic healings, also. You cannot deal with millions of people practicing spiritual mind healing and not have obvious cures that would have been cured anyway, even if they had never heard of God. The person on the outside says, "This man would have recovered anyway, Doctor." He might have. But there are many cases where that can't be said. There are times when the case cannot be refuted, where the patient was healed without medical assistance, or with it, accompanied by a metaphysical Practitioner.

This has been made obvious in the United States since 1875 by the development of the Christian Science church, which has been one of the greatest sources for good in the awakening of the public mind to healing that we have had on this planet. I am not an exponent of that organization, but I appreciate what it has done in awakening the world to the understanding that God heals man. There can be no question as to its extent, its influence, and the good that it has done.

The world in general, however, does not know that concurrently with the Christian Science Movement there have been other metaphysical teachings developed that covered the same ground, and in their own way have done as much healing. They have never acquired the national prominence that the Christian Science church has, for they never organized sufficiently to get it.

In the United States today, outside of Christian Science, whose influence I have no way of knowing, there are between five and ten million people reading our literature. You may say, "That is a drop in the bucket." No, it is not, because minorities are always more powerful than majorities. Never worry about the majority; worry about the minority because they are troublemakers. Minority groups are always powerful groups.

Five to ten million people, excluding Christian Science, are an effective minority. In the United State of America today, there are over 2,000 churches of New Thought. This is something to be reckoned with.

How does metaphysics heal? In Religious Science, healing should be as automatic as in any other phase or function of life. We believe that the health of the individual is spiritual in origin. It comes from a Cause beyond our explanation. As we study health, we see it as the operation of Intelligence, and it responds to intelligence.

What do you do when you feel run down? You plan an intelligent program to be built up. When you are ill you do the same thing, and your body responds. The universe, including man, is the function of an Intelligence that is greater than any single individual unit of It.

God is mind, or a basic creative Power, a creative Intelligence that is always active, and we name it Life. It is a knowingness in motion. It is Something that knows, and as It knows, It moves upon Itself, and creation is the result. Thomas Troward writes that creation is the result of the self-contemplation of God, meaning that the infinite Mind contemplating Itself moves upon Itself, and form appears.

You exist in a creative field of mind action. The orthodox systems of religion teach the separation of God and man, and therefore cannot understand scientific spiritual healing. To them, if a person is healed by prayer, it is due to a special intercession, or due to a miracle either by God or by some lesser deity from another plan of action. When Orthodoxy established that God is God and man is man, and drew the line between saying that God was good and man was a sinner, they robbed their own organizations of the power to heal.

In Religious Science, we do not heal through intercession. We heal by calm, clear knowing, because we are dealing with a Power that is Life, a Power that responds to intelligence, which is only impeded by us. We always stand in our own way. We always stand in our own light. We always make our own mistakes. We are always cluttered with our own false opinions. It is apparent that disease in all its forms is due to interior confusion in man, and healing is accomplished by the clearing of this interior confusion.

That is what we teach. That is what we believe, and that is what we practice. Does it work? Yes. How do you do it? You begin by knowing something you do not know now. You say, "How on earth can I do that?" In the sixth grade you didn't know advanced mathematics. You didn't know geometry. How did you gradually know it? You studied it. How did you study it? You studied it with other people. What did you do? You read books. You listened while teachers explained it to you. Suddenly you knew geometry.

In the congregation this morning, 90 percent of the people know exactly what I am talking about and have proved it to themselves. How did they do it? They studied spiritual healing. Where did they study it? Here or in other New Thought churches. How did they do it? They said, "I don't know if it works, but this man says it does, so I will listen to him. I'll read the books he recommends, and then I'll know." That is what they did. Then, they went to work on their own minds.

Try this the next time you have a cold, and you will know. Try it the next time your little old friend the virus comes visiting. You won't know that Healing is true because I say it. You won't know it because books by important authors say it. You will only know mental healing when you do it. You only know mathematics when you use mathematics. You only know multiplication when you are using multiplication. The rest of the time these are only latent memories in your subconscious mind.

You go to a grocery store and buy three pounds of coffee. Coffee is 94 cents a pound, and you start thinking, "Okay, 3 times 94 is $2.82." You practiced mathematics. How did you do it? You maneuvered your mind and memory until you knew something you didn't know before. You activated your mind until you knew an idea that you had not known before.

That is exactly how you practice mental healing. It is that simple. You start with a simple proposition. (I am sure this is the way Jesus healed), that God and man are not separate—they are one function. The deity isn't in one location and you in another. You are in Life, and this Divine Life is in you. You are in an Intelligence, and this Intelligence is in you. Whatever the nature of God is, It is what It is at the point where you are. Whatever the Infinite knows, It knows it at the point in space that you occupy. Whatever the Infinite is, It is where you are, and it is what you are. You cannot relegate the Creative Power to a distance and expect to live in comfort and health.

The individual is the action of God, the action of Life. Religious Science is not interested in your sins. It is not interested in your mistakes, your past, or in your present. It is not interested in your medical history, political history, or financial history. It is interested in one thing: *THE INDIVIDUAL IS AN INLET AND AN OUTLET OF LIFE. THIS LIFE,*

OF WHICH THE INDIVIDUAL IS THE INLET AND THE OUTLET, IS A LIFE WHICH HAS WITHIN IT THE CAPACITY TO RESTORE ITSELF.

If you cut your finger, it is healed because an Intelligence within you knows how to heal it. Take that same idea and expand it to any illness of the body. The cut finger you didn't worry about. You're used to being healed in minor ways. But the pain in your stomach, what do you do about it? Immediately you blame it on something you ate. Before the pain has registered for two minutes, you are certain you have an ulcer. At the end of ten minutes of speculation on evil, you are certain you have a cancer. Isn't that right? You jumped into a mass of negative speculation, an area of negative thought. You accepted it, believed it, and started to be ready for it. Now that you have pain, it means you shouldn't visit the Smiths on Tuesday night. They serve rich foods, and you had better stay on tea and toast. This pain shows that your ulcer is developing nicely; you mustn't accept dinner invitations.

That is exactly what we do to ourselves. We look at a cut finger and know it will only be a matter of two weeks for it to be perfect. Why? Because you let an Intelligence you respect function in Its normal way. Yet, the moment the greater pain appeared, you did everything mentally you could to impede Life's normal operation. You jumped into fear, negative speculation, and false diagnosis. You ran the whole gamut of negative emotions. You said, "I studied Religious Science for three years, and it doesn't work." You studied it, but you didn't practice it. There is a difference between studying and practicing. I once knew geometry, but I no longer practice it. I couldn't now if I wanted to.

When illness affects you in a slight or major form, go to work on it affirmatively in your own mind as quickly, specifically, and warmly as you jump into negative speculation. Doing this, you will probably never be sick another day in your life.

Spiritual Mind healing is applying common sense at the level of mind action. It is keeping the mind clear so the Divine Intelligence, which is the nature of God in man, can operate intelligently with no obstacles and no impediments. That is scientific spiritual mind healing.

You may say, "Dr. Barker, that isn't the way I understood it. I thought you sat down and made affirmations." You do. That is our technique to keep your mind straight. Spiritual affirmations are necessary as a way to clear your mind. I use them whenever I have to clear my mind due to an emotional disturbance, a pain, or the pain of someone else. When I can't think straight, I sit down and do my spiritual work. It clears my thought.

The advantage of learning affirmations is that it takes the beginner's mind and saturates it with positive statements that remain in the memory field. These rise to the surface and can be used at any time the individual needs them the rest of his life. I have probably memorized more affirmations than anyone else in this Church. It is a part of my work to do so. I wouldn't give anything for the spiritual storehouse that I have available at the drop of a hat.

When a negative condition presents itself either in me or in a person I want to help, I turn to That within me which doesn't know, recognize, or indulge in evil. I am not interested in negative speculations on the problem. I listen to them, but I am not interested in them. I am interested in the person who tells me, for I am interested in people. I am not interested in the negative itself.

The "mumbo-jumbo" that critics emphasize when they take potshots at us is a very healthy thing. It equips you at the subconscious level to meet negatives with positives.

Does God do the healing? Yes. It would seem as if our technique is self-healing. Where is God in the picture? God is the whole picture. For God is the life, the substance, and the intelligence that does it. God is the will in the person that does it. God is the substance of the very flesh in which the healing takes place.

Spiritual Mind healing is a fact. It is a practice. It is definite. It will find its proper place in the world. The day will come when medicine and religion will work together. They are vaguely starting. There are the few places where it is tried. But, attempts are still vague. The average member of the medical profession still thinks that Christian Science, Religious Science, and Unity Practitioners are pleasant people who ought to find something else to do. Unfortunately, we must heal because scientific spiritual healing works. The healed are many. The unhappy who are changed into gladness are many. The dispirited, the forlorn, push their shoulders back and look at life instead of shrinking away from it. God is in man as man responds, as man recognizes his own divine nature.

CHAPTER 8

BLESSED ARE THE RIGHT-MINDED

RELIGIOUS SCIENCE is a system of spiritual thinking premised on a Divine Mind. We do not teach the theological salvation of souls because we don't know what that term means. We know, however, that the individual who has an inner tone of inspiration and follows through on it always comes out right. The Wise, the Great, the True, and the Fine have always taught one simple proposition: Handle ideas rightly, and life will always adjust. Buddha, Isaiah, and Jesus said it. The Psalms and the Sermon on the Mount tell it, for they say the same thing.

Religion is the individual's acknowledgment of his own Divine potential. It is the recognition that the inner man is always greater than his outer experience. In you is

Something that is always greater than what you are experiencing. Your material experience is necessarily conditioned by your five senses. But, in you is That which is greater than your five senses. Your five senses tell you where you are, but they never tell you what you are. That is why Jesus cautioned you about them. Your five senses tell you where you are, but not what you are. Spiritually alert people have always been more interested in what they were than where they were.

Ask yourself, "Am I more interested in where I am in life than what I am? Am I only interested in pleasing my five senses?" What I see I like, what I hear I like, what I taste I like, what I touch and what I smell I like. I can live in a beautiful home. I can eat what I like. I can smell beautiful flowers. I can wear luxurious clothes to touch.

You can always arrange your five-sense world. Anyone can. Jesus and people like him did not worry about their outer world, for they knew that when people really want to change it, they can. If you don't like where you are living, you can move. You may say, "I have been looking for an apartment for two years and can't find one." Most people who look for an apartment for two years and can't find one don't really want to move. If you don't like your clothes, buy new ones. You can arrange your five-sense world around you. Jesus did. He always had what he wanted when he wanted it. He wasn't cluttered with things when he didn't want them. He lived with ease in his five-sense world. You also can do that.

Living with ease in a five-sense world does not satisfy. Every person has an inner hunger. In the Sermon on the Mount, it states that the people who hunger and thirst after righteousness shall be filled. They realize that the five-sense world is a pleasant place in which to live, but that it isn't the full answer to life. I am glad I am alive. I like this life. You probably like where you are. If not, you would not stay there. You would do something about it.

If you are in Life and appreciate Life, you are actually seeking a deeper consciousness. You are saying, "Here is my world, and it is well arranged. It gets out of kilter now and then. This stupid thing happens, and that unpleasant thing happens. But, my life is fairly well regulated. Yet, I don't feel complete." Why? Because the inward path of spiritual investigation is a path you must take through your own mind. You can follow a leader. That is easy. But, this world is always in need of original thinking.

Every society and culture must have original thinkers to survive. That brings the question: Are you an original thinker? This question only you can answer. Most people are not. They accept new ideas, but the new ideas were developed by someone else. They buy the newest things, but these things arose in the minds of other thinkers.

I often tell the fair sex that the hats they will wear at

Easter are already made. The hats are in the stores waiting for them. Last summer a designer fashioned them. Last fall they were manufactured, and now they are packed in the warehouses. About the 15th of March, women start their Easter search. They walk into a shop, and there is the right hat. It is there because someone had an original thought. Yet, someone else did the new thinking, unless you make your own hats.

Spirit is that which causes the individual to be a participant in life. Spirit is that in you which causes you to function. It is an inner demand.

You have to be what you are. You don't have to be where you are. It is your nature to think and to feel, and this you can't stop, you can only direct. Choose to do original thinking. You wouldn't have a Bible if people had not thought to originate it. You would not have the latest novel if someone hadn't had an original thought. Always, there is original thinking. The blessed people are those who occasionally have an original thought.

It is not easy to have an original thought when everything is "canned" for us. It is easier to buy a new cookbook than to originate a recipe. Yet, we search for interesting restaurants that have unusual recipes. We spend our money to buy the unique, and all the time we could be unique ourselves.

The right-minded people are those who live at the point where they are and seek a deeper meaning to life. They live with honesty, integrity, and justice. Constantly ask yourself: "Is there a Spiritual something on the inside of me that I can quicken and stimulate?"

"Dr. Barker, can you really find God?" No, you never completely find Infinite Mind. Do you ever get to heaven? No, you never completely get there. Then why tell us to do it?" Because you must seek it. You never explore it fully, but you uncover a great part of it. You never complete the journey, yet you go far on the road. Whatever this Thing is deep underneath, It is a Thing that compels your interest. It says, "Follow thou me." It says, "Come unto me." It says, "Seek and ye shall find. Knock and the door shall be opened." We are never complete, yet we are always seeking completion. We become complete in the seeking of It.

Is this practical? Yes, it is. Why is it practical? Look at Life from more than a five-sense viewpoint and develop an inner stability. You will develop an inner buoyancy, an inner calmness, and an inner joy.

You look through the atmosphere of your own mind. You accomplish everything by thinking about it. How will you go to a restaurant after this service? You will do it by thinking about it.

How do you find God in the midst of you? By thinking about It. Not by thinking that you don't know God, but by thinking that you do. Believing you know It, you know It. You are dealing with a Power that responds to the impulse you give It. The Infinite is forever resting in silent repose. It waits. The person you ought to be, you are. Perfect Self indwells you, and it awaits your recognition. You do It by believing that It is.

Declare that you believe that within you is a Spiritual Potential, a Greatness that you have never started to tap. Believe that this Power in you is more important than you have ever realized It to be.

You can arrange your outer world. You can live within your budget. You can live within your usual framework of friends and social life. You can make those adjustments. But, within you is Something that is the very source of Life itself.

We have sought God everywhere except at a logical point within. We have sought God on the holy mountain, in the great cathedral and in nature. But we have never looked within ourselves. As you understand the operation of consciousness, your mind and emotions, you know that you never see outside of you anything you haven't first known within you. You will never find the God outside until you have first found the God within. You will never find peace, harmony, order, or health on the outside until you first have them on the inside.

How do you do this? You do it by saying you have them. You do it by knowing that you are a part of all Life. You are a part of God. You are a part of everything that is good. That is where you place your attention. Evil falls apart when it starves to death for lack of attention. Evil dies when you don't feed it. There isn't a negative in your world that will not go if you diminish your interest in it.

"I worried all last night." You didn't at all. You probably slept at least six out of the eight hours. You mean that when you went to bed, you went on a nice worry jag because you had nothing else to think about. You went to bed last night and worried. When you woke up this morning, you felt miserable. Why wouldn't you? You tell everyone about it, and they feel sorry for you.

I don't go to bed to worry. I go to bed to sleep. You say, "I could not help worrying." You could if you read our books. Just don't go to bed. If you are going to worry, do it sitting up.

Blessed are the people who seek a Center within them to balance the activity of the senses without. Blessed are those who know that Life is for the living. Life is for the person who can act in balance and create something from an original thought. If you live for your job, you are wrong. If you live for a person, you are wrong. If you live for your family, you are equally wrong. Life was never created to be limited that way. You live with the person and for the person, but you live for Life. You live for your family and with your family, but you live in a larger creative atmosphere than merely that. You work, but work is the healthy outlet of energy for the production of income. You never die of overwork. You die of the tensions created within you while resisting work.

Life is for the person who can grasp it. You don't live it by getting sensation from the outside. If more money would make a perfect life, that would be easy. If the right apartment would do it, that would be simple. If friends and loved ones would do it, that would be easy, too. These don't do it.

Within you is Something born not of the flesh, nor of the will of man, but of the Spirit. God matters not what you call Him. It matters not how long you seek Him, or whether you find Him in fullness. You will find so much of God that you will leave with greater ease.

CHAPTER 9

WHY I DO NOT BELIEVE IN REINCARNATION

NINETY PERCENT of the people reading this booklet believe in reincarnation. Many will purchase it because they want a mental argument. They will not be the least bit convinced when they have finished reading it. They will still believe in re-embodiment. Religious Science has little to do with reincarnation. Religious Science leaves each person free to decide such things for himself.

I speak on this subject because many people have asked me to do it. When I first came to New York in 1945, I did not believe in reincarnation. Many argued with me about the idea, and for three years I thought I did believe in it. Lately, the more I have thought about it, the more convinced I have become that I do not believe in it. This is the last time I will switch conclusions. But, you may believe in reincarnation, for you are a free agent.

Reincarnation is one of the oldest religious beliefs. It is very ancient and was believed long before the Bible was written. It is interesting that the Jews did not include it as part of their doctrine. They may not have included it for the very simple reason that it was an obvious belief in the times in which they lived. If we were writing a Bible today, we would not bother to include the alphabet, nor the table of mathematics. We would assume that everyone knew these. That may be the reason why Reincarnation is not in the Old Testament.

Other ancient religions did write a great deal about it. You will find Reincarnation in ancient Egypt and in all oriental scriptures. It is the basis of Buddhism, the largest religion in the present world. Two-thirds of the people living on the earth today believe in reincarnation.

Christianity is quite unique in that it does not teach reincarnation. You may not realize that Christianity is not the most important religion in the world as far as numbers are concerned. It is one of the most important religions, but only one of several. There are far more Buddhists in the world than there are Christians.

Reincarnation is very ancient in origin and has been believed by many of the greatest minds who have ever lived. It has been accepted as a fundamental principle by people who didn't merely accept a theology or believe because a Church said it was so. They believed it because from their own experience they felt it was true.

People trying to convince me of reincarnation say that the fact that two-thirds of the people living on earth since the beginning of recorded history believe it makes it true. That doesn't make it true to me. They feel that if it is ancient and has been the core of many religions, it is therefore true. That still doesn't convince me. If that alone made it factual, then we should go back to witchcraft for our medicine. An idea that has existed for 10,000 years is not necessarily a truth. Because millions of people believe an idea does not make it a truth. It is still a belief, even though an understandable one.

Jesus believed in reincarnation. In Matthew 17:10–13, he said that John the Baptist was the reincarnation of Elijah. You can't find the word *reincarnation,* but you can find where he says "Elijah is come already, and they knew him not." Then he mentions John the Baptist.

Reincarnation states that you and I come back here, so we have to define what "here" is. I must know where I am, if I am to return to it. You may reply that "here" is very obvious; it is a planet called Earth, revolving around the sun. Is it? Today, physics is no longer a material science. It is a philosophical and mathematical science. Only in rare instances does modern physics deal with the factual material world. Many present-day physicists tell you in their books and lectures that the present material universe is nothing but waves of energy locked up in temporary form.

When the atom was first explored, it was discovered that each atom was a world in itself. You have never seen an atom, because no one has ever seen an atom. No scientist, though he can explode them, has ever seen an atom. Yet, he knows what they are and what is in them, that while they do not exist for the five senses, they do exist at the level of wavelengths of energy.

The present universe in which I exist is a universe of mind action. I am the perceiver of my world. The universe is nothing but energy locked up in a temporary form. In the final analysis, it is nothing but waves of energy operating at certain wavelengths, and that is all it is.

You may answer that I can't explain the universe out of existence so easily. Let me tell you something. Each time you dream, you are in a definite world, and while you are in it, it is as real to you as is the world in which you function when you are awake. Your dream world as you dream is as real to you as this auditorium, the chair in which you are seated, and the speaker in front of you. Remember this the next time you dream. Tonight before going to sleep, say to yourself, "I want to dream and I want to know when I am dreaming that it is a dream."

You will discover that you CAN know when you are dreaming and also realize that it is a dream. This is interesting to do. You become aware that "you" in the dream state is no different than "you" in the waking state, except for one thing: In the dream state there is neither past, present, nor future in the sense of separated time. Time does not exist in a dream. You can be with your grandmother one minute, in the office where you were this afternoon another minute, and where you were on your vacation in another split second.

In the dream state, there is neither space nor time. Yet while you are in it, that dream state is exactly as objective, as real, as your present state. For example, you have eaten meals in dreams; you have drunk water. You have felt it going down your throat as water. Every sensation you have in the waking state, you can have in a sleep state during dreams. I want to make this clear—your dream world at the time you are in it is exactly as real as your material world is while you are awake.

What did you do? You went to sleep. You shifted from the series of energy wavelengths where you know form, weight, density, time, and space, to a dream state where there is form, but not weight, density, time, and space.

Years ago at Unity School in Kansas City, I remember Charles Fillmore telling a class in advanced metaphysics that he believed that if 51 percent of the people on this planet at any instant really believed that the universe was Mind in action, that the material world would disappear. That doesn't prove it so, but a wise man made that statement.

The present material universe is the automatic result of man's belief in the necessity of material form, weight, and density. When you die, the one thing you miss is solidity, weight, and density. You are not my mind projected, and I am not your mind projected. We are all living, but what we are calling "here" is not the world that is really here.

As metaphysicians, we say that man is consciousness. Life is consciousness. Body is consciousness objected as form. If my body is my consciousness, then I carry my body with me because I carry consciousness with me. Therefore, I will never be out of body.

You will have a body after death because you carry your body idea with you. You will always have a world around you because you carry your world with you. Psychics tell us that when a person dies and wakes on the next plane, he does not know he is dead. You may have seen the *Topper* movies. The whole story is there. When you awaken, wherever it is, you do not know you have died. You do not know that you have gone anywhere. Why? Because you carry your present consciousness with you. A person who passes out of his body when he is sick awakens on the next plane surrounded by the same atmosphere. If he died in a hospital room, he wakes up in a hospital room on the next plane.

The Infinite Mind has never duplicated anything. There are not two boards in a floor alike. There are not two hairs in your head alike. The universe never repeats itself. Whatever the Creative Spirit is, It makes all things new. It always makes all things different and unique. God has never duplicated Itself once. Why should It duplicate you? If the Infinite is a progressive, creative, forward movement, then why do you have to come back?

You may argue with me that coming back is really going forward. Well, that is a play on words. I am intrigued by the metaphysicians who are ardent believers in reincarnation. I say to them, you know, don't you, that Jesus believed in reincarnation? Yes. Well, do you believe in the second coming of Christ the way the Fundamentalists do? No, I don't. I believe the second coming of Christ is the revelation of Truth in the individual soul. Yet, you believe in reincarnation, and that Jesus believed in reincarnation, but you do not believe he is coming back. Does it make sense?

Jesus did believe in reincarnation. He said definitely that he was coming back. You can metaphysicalize it, you can "allegorialize" it. He said he was coming back. But, he didn't.

You may say to me, "But, when you arrive at a certain stage of spiritual understanding, you do not have to return." Well, he apparently did not know that. Bible scholars say that the reason the Four Gospels were written as late as they were was that the writers did not bother to write about a man they expected to return at any minute. His disciples really believed he was coming back, but he didn't.

The universe is an endless, progressive system. "In my Father's house are many mansions" (John 14:2). You move from wavelength to wavelength. You do not need to come back here, because you take "here" with you. Every experience, the most minute detail that you have been aware of since you were born, is in you now, and you take it with you. You need not return, because you carry it all there—wherever "there" is.

All that I am, I shall be forevermore. Each time I die, I move forward, as Paul said, "from glory to glory. Forgetting those things which are behind and reaching forth unto those things which are before, I press toward the mark of my high calling" (Philippians 3:13). I cannot stand still. I cannot go back. I must go forward.

You take "here" with you, because you are consciousness. Consciousness as man is also consciousness omnipresent. You are the image and likeness of God. God is everywhere, so you are everywhere. You are not everywhere as body, but you are everywhere as consciousness. Right now you are in Buckingham Palace and at the South Pole, but you do not realize it. As consciousness, you are everywhere. Body is merely an operating point, the present material belief you are holding. As that, it is very important, but you could be as well off without it. Religions have told their followers that they will survive their physical bodies, because they carry their body-idea with them.

One of the reasons reincarnation has such a tremendous following is that people love to glorify the past. We also have a tendency to stand still in the present and a reluctance to move ahead. It is easier to remember what I did last year than to think about what I will do tomorrow. The past is known and is therefore comfortable. We try to remain static in the present, because it is easy. We hesitate to investigate the future, for it is unknown. Yet, every religion has told us of the future, and beckoned us toward it. They have proclaimed the future to be good and that it was independent of the past. The basis of orthodox Christianity is the cleansing of sin, the getting rid of the past. This is also the basis of modern psychology. Be rid of the past in order to move forward. But, the tendency of the Reincarnationist is to want to come back to something he already knows. Yet, God never made anything twice.

I cannot see any reason for returning. Going ahead is wonderful. Why do you want to return here and do it all over again? You can progress right now. If you say that I must correct every mistake I have ever made, I agree with you. But I don't have to come back here to do it. If you tell me that I must gradually evolve my consciousness through spiritual development, I agree with you. But must I come back here to do it? Many believe that you must return to wipe out karmic debts. I doubt if you know how many karmic debts you have already wiped out in this existence. People tell me the tragedies of their lives. As I listen, I think they wipe out more karmic debts in the present life than they know.

We came from a lower wavelength; we are now at this wavelength; we will go to a higher wavelength. We do not move from matter to mind and back to matter. We move from consciousness to a higher level of consciousness, to another higher level of consciousness.

If you believe in reincarnation, you have accepted your pattern to come back, go through the hard job of being born, the tragedy of childhood, adolescence, youth, maturity, and old age. You always demonstrate what you believe. The danger of believing in a philosophy that will bring you back to your present universe is that you will do it if you believe it. I won't return because I do not believe it. It is the Law of Life that I demonstrate my belief.

If you want to come back here, come back. But, you won't find me here your next trip around. Be certain that the reason you want to come back is not merely that you are afraid of going ahead. Coming back is easy; it is the known. Moving courageously ahead is never easy, but Life demands that you do it.

Believe in reincarnation if you choose. God made you free. I do not believe in reincarnation, and I shall not come back.

CHAPTER 10

WHY I BELIEVE IN LIFE AFTER DEATH

I BELIEVE in life after death because it makes sense. I cannot conceive of my own non-existence. I cannot believe an intelligent God would create an individual, cause this individual to go through experiences until he is really of value to his world, and then demand his complete disintegration.

Few of us are worth much to the world until we are past the age of 50. We go through the process of learning to where we are more or less matured, and our wisdom is somewhat balanced. Situations that warped us at the age of 20 no longer warp us at 50, 60, 70, or 80. We arrive at some "common sense" and, all of a sudden, off we go.

An intelligent Creative Process would not suddenly

extinguish permanently Its highest form of creation. Studying evolution you realize that we have come a long way. If I did not believe in life after death, I would stop working today and exist on Public Welfare. Why should I work 8 to 12 hours a day, have the headaches, the bother, and the trouble of running a church? I wouldn't be bothered with it if I did not think I was creating something that was a permanent, valuable addition to life, including a contribution to my own continuous life.

The reason you and I have our goals and work hard in our jobs is because we have a sense of a future. Not merely a future here, because your material future on this earth is temporary. There is no security in the material universe, and there never has been. If you don't think so, remember the money that was lost in the Depression of 1929.

I believe that after death I will not be very different than I am now. You may ask if I believe in heaven and hell. No, I don't. You say, "But the Bible says you go to either heaven or hell." I don't think it does. I am suspicious that I have read the Bible more than the average person. I have studied it from all angles. I cannot find the instruction in it that orthodoxy claims is there.

You can read into your Bible anything you want to read into it. If you want to find heaven and hell in your Bible, there are references to them. I don't think the Bible teaches heaven and hell. But, I do think it teaches life after death. I don't know a person today who is spiritually, emotionally, mentally, or in any other way equipped to function in the old-fashioned heaven, if there really was one. You wouldn't know how to live in a world where there was nothing to do. I cannot believe that an Infinite Intelligence would make me work so hard here, and then suddenly never work again throughout eternity. Nor can I believe in hell, because the universe is not a system of punishment.

We exist in a universe that permits us to be what we want to be. Consciously or subconsciously, we are what we want to be. You may protest that you are not what you want to be. But, sit in the office of a psychologist for three hours, and he will assure you that you are exactly where you ought to be because of what you are, because of the consistent action and reaction of your mentality. We are free here, and we are free hereafter. No Deity binds us through eternity.

There is an endless progression of Life. If I were to drop dead at this instant, I would not know it. In my own mind I would still be speaking to you in Town Hall. Why? Because that is what I believe I am doing now. The most interesting thing, which people who have investigated the problem of life after death have told us, is that no one changes by dying. You can't change one iota.

If you were in deep melancholia and said, "I'd like to die," and did, you would still be in melancholia. Wherever you go, when you get there, you will be exactly the same as when you left here. There is no improvement in death. That is very important, because we have had such false beliefs about this. Your grandfather, on the next plane, unless he had changed since you last saw him, is exactly the way he was on this one. I happen to have had a very unpleasant grandfather. He was a tartar, and I imagine still is. At least, he didn't change for 75 years here, and he has been over there about 30. If he didn't change here in 75 years, I doubt he has changed where he is now.

You do not improve by dying, so you had better improve now. You will be exactly the same person as you were the day you stepped out of your body. You should not fear death for one great simple reason: You do not fear life. Whatever God is, It is everywhere. Being everywhere, then you are never out of the Presence, whether you are here or somewhere else.

If you were to board a boat and go to an isolated port on a distant continent, people who said goodbye to you might weep. Yet, you would know that where you went, you would be all right. There would be lodging, food, and people around you. In whatever town you arrive, you would eventually find your way and feel at home. You might find it difficult for a while to get adjusted to a new language, new types of people, and different reactions from people. Perhaps there aren't movies, television, and radios in this place. But gradually you would fall into the village life pattern. You would make friends. You would receive and give affection and warmth. You would find creative things to do. That is exactly what happens when you step out of your present body.

The "you" that you take to this new location is the same "you" that left New York on the boat. The "you" that you will be on the next plane is the same "you" that you are now. You do not improve by dying. Neither do you retrogress. You remain the same because Life is a continuity.

When you die, what dies and what goes where? After you die, your relatives go through the barbaric ritual of having a funeral. Luckily, you don't know this. You are much better off by not knowing it, for many people who haven't liked you for years come to look at you and say how wonderful you were. People who couldn't abide you send flowers.

What in you doesn't die? Your body apparently does. The great mystics, saints, sages, prophets—of all religious beliefs from both the East and West—agree that there is a body within the body. Your present physical body is not your real body.

Psychics name your real body the *etheric body*. In Religious Science we call it *consciousness*, because we discovered that what you think, you think through the entire body. Most people believe that they think in their heads. That is only the focal point, as the heart is the center of circulation, the lungs the center of respiration, and the stomach the center of digestion. You do not think with your mind; your mind thinks, and what your mind thinks, you think throughout. Consciousness is not locked up in gray matter. Consciousness extends throughout the entire body. Your etheric body is exactly the same as your material body, except it is about an inch larger. It stands out around you about an inch.

You do not live in a body; your body lives in you. The physical body is inside your consciousness. It is inside your etheric body, and with death the physical body separates from the etheric body, and you in the etheric body move on. You take your mental body with you. That is one of the meanings of the theological dogma of ascension. We all take our mental bodies with us. You take your consciousness, and your consciousness is in the form of a body.

If you have never investigated psychic matters, you say "poppycock." If you have studied along these lines, you know that what I am saying is probably true. I spent one entire year in a psychic phenomena group. I knew the people in that group. I knew the leader of that group. What took place was neither imagination nor hallucination. What took place was fact to me. Someone else might go through the same experience and say that it was a bunch of nonsense. But, the field of psychic phenomena has, without a shadow of a doubt, proven the continuity of life.

Should you try to communicate with those who have gone on? I don't think so. Leave them alone. They are busy and happy, so why bother them? I see no reason for bothering my father and mother, both of whom are somewhere. I have work to do. I have friends. I have loved ones. I have people for whom I care. I have outlets for giving and receiving affection, giving and receiving interest. I have much to do in my work right now. So, why bother my father and mother? You may answer that the reason you would bother them is to be certain they are all right. Well, my parents got along all right while they were here. They had common sense. They lived healthy, efficient, practical, sensible lives, so I am assuming they know how to get along where they are.

Everyone wants to know about life after death, but they always want it to agree with their own set opinions. Try to convince anyone of a new idea of life after death, and you have a hard job. People want the old-fashioned heaven, which makes life easy, or the old-fashioned hell, which takes care of the people they hate. This is a very convenient theological arrangement.

Where does your body of consciousness go? I don't think it goes anywhere. I think it stays where it is. I believe all planes interpenetrate one another. There may be 5,000 Town Halls right on this site, just as there are 200 radio programs in this auditorium, and 50 television programs. We don't know they are here. How do we know there aren't 500 town halls right here? Perhaps every concert that has ever been given here is still being given. Just because our eyes can't see all this, that doesn't mean anything. The five senses are the most unreliable information channels in the world.

You can't see the next plane. It is good that you can't. I am glad I don't know from where I came or where I am going. My present life is filled with creative work, and I am content.

Where do you go? Life is one system within another, and you merely move from one wavelength to another. Like the radio, you turn from one station to another and change programs. I think you do that when you die.

It is the general consensus of psychic researchers that when you die you awaken in a healthy body. Probably when you awaken, you will be in a misty atmosphere, as though there were a fog. You will wonder where you are. But, you will sense that you feel well. After a while, you will realize that you aren't in a material world, because you can sit in a chair when you want to, but you can also walk through it when you want to. Suddenly you realize: I must be dead.

This fact is important. Knowing this when it happens to you, you will realize all the sooner that you have died. At the same instant, you feel as though you are not dead at all. You feel alive. You will be busy beginning new activities.

Will you see people? Yes, you will see people. You will talk to people. You will eat with people. Will you meet people that you have loved? Yes, you will. But, you will find them a bit changed. After all, being away from you may have changed them a little. But, also being away from them, you have changed, too.

You will see the people you want to see. You will do the things you want to do if you are equipped to do them. If you have never sung on this plane, you will not be an opera singer on the next. If you have never played golf on this plane, you won't suddenly make a hole in one on the next plane. You are "you," wherever you go, and you don't change. Yet, there are as many opportunities to change on the next plane as there are here as time unfolds.

On the next plane, you will go where you belong by right of your consciousness, just as here. There is a law of mental gravitation that places you where you belong. Divine Law works here; It works there.

"Will I be happy on the next plane?" is a question people often ask. You will be as happy as you are here. But, there is a difference. Completely materially minded people aren't happy on the next plane. People who have developed their consciousness spiritually, who are interested in spiritual ideas, who have developed their cultural senses—these are the happiest people on the next plane. The complete materialist is unhappy, for on the next plane making money doesn't mean a thing. Eating, drinking, and having recreation are not the primary goals. If you live to eat, drink, and have fun, you are at a loss over there—you have to adjust.

You can go to any public library and read eight hours a day for two years and never read all the books on this subject written by intelligent people. I don't mean crackpots. Life after death is not the belief of a person, or the belief of any one religion. Every religion has defined eternal continuity. Varying religions have had different revelations about it.

In the last hundred years, an extensive study has been made of psychics by intelligent, distinguished people who have had amazing experiences. There is a great field of psychic literature in which, if you care to investigate, you could find out everything I am telling you. I have spent years, not only thinking about life after death, but reading about it.

You don't have to believe in Life after Death to practice Religious Science. But I'll tell you one thing. Liberalize your concept of the hereafter to some extent, and you will find it much easier when you get there.

Life never changes quickly. The baby does not become an adult overnight. No person achieves great works quickly. You earn everything you get on this plane, and you must earn it on the next. That is one of the most spiritual statements that can be made. I am glad that the God who created me leaves me free to discover myself. I am free to experiment with life. I can grow, develop, expand, evolve here and in the endless continuity of the hereafter. That is the glory and the greatness of God.

CHAPTER 11

FEAR IS IGNORANCE

Opening Remarks

WE BELIEVE in Something that is taking place right here and right now. We are not interested in how It worked in the past, nor are we concerned about how It will work in the future. We are dealing with the present action of God.

"For thine is the kingdom, and the power, and the glory, forever. Amen." This is a positive definition of a present action. For thine is, not was, the kingdom, the power, and the glory. In Religious Science, we are dealing with a Mind that is thinking right now. We are dealing with a Power that is in action right now.

The Bible in our Western culture, and other great books in the Eastern culture, give us the history of what It has done up until now. This gives us a sense of well-being. If God did all this in other times, then God can do what It does in the now. We are in a present God, a present Intelligence, a present Life, a present Health, a present Peace, a present Action. Because we are in It, we can be aware of It. When we are aware of It, we have the experience of It.

At the moment, I may know how much money I have in my wallet, but I can reach into my pocket, take out the wallet, count the bills, and know how much I have. Therefore, I can, if I choose, use the money. Being aware of it, I have it.

That is what we are doing in this church. We are training our minds to be aware that at every split second there is a fullness of life to be lived. There is a totality of goodness to be experienced. Right now—not last week—we are aware of It, right here and right now. You are seated here in Town Hall, and I am standing here in Town Hall. There is nothing mystical about it. There is nothing strange or occult. There is nothing peculiar. Whatever God is, It is here; It is now; It is as we think; It is as we feel.

I always like to tell you the story when, years ago, I had my telephone listed. A woman called me at eight o'clock one Sunday morning, which is one of the reasons why I no longer have a listed telephone number. She said,

"Dr. Barker, my cousin Ella is in town, and she said she will come to church with me this morning. I have one request to ask. Will you for one Sunday please not call God 'It.' My cousin will not understand this. She is used to a real man-God, up in heaven looking down on her, writing in a book everything that she does wrong. Please don't call God 'It'."

After the service, I went out into the lobby of Town Hall and was properly introduced to Cousin Ella, and she told me in a sincere voice that she was helped by the service and enjoyed it. However, I am sure that I called God "It" during the lecture.

You who are used to me know why I am doing this. We are not dealing with a man-God, nor are we dealing with a woman-God. Many ancient religions had their gods and goddesses. We are dealing with that Principle out of which both masculinity and femininity proceed. We are dealing with That which becomes Its own creation. We are existing in this creation. We are rejoicing in It. We people this morning are not fighting the world. We are using the world. We are not here to battle sin. We are here to live the life that proceeds victoriously.

"For thine is the kingdom," right here, right now. "Thine is the power," which is in action in your thought and mine, right now. "Thine is the glory," the expansion, the fullness of life. Let us be still a moment and take this into our minds.

The Treatment

THERE is but One God, One Spirit, One Truth, One Life, One Reality, not somewhere, but here. It is in our present thought. It is in our present body. It is in our present feelings. Its Presence is that of Peace and Order, Good Will, Harmony, Right Action, Inspiration, right here and right now.

The Sermon

I AM TALKING today on the subject, "Fear Is Ignorance," and that is all it is. The only thing you are afraid of is the one you don't understand. The minute you understand a situation, you are no longer afraid of it. This is why your fears differ at every age level. At every age level, you have a different set of fears. As you mature from one level to the next level, you drop one set of fears and take on another set. As a baby, you were afraid of many things that you are not afraid of now. As a teenager, you were afraid of many things that you are not afraid of now.

You need to assess what you are afraid of now because your fears will lead you into self-discovery, provided you analyze them correctly, provided you look upon them as an asset, because they are an asset. Anything that might cause fear in you today is an asset to you, provided you do something creative about it. Fear is ignorance, and you do not need to be ignorant. There is no reason why you should continue to be ignorant in any subject. Do some research in the matter. Find out what is happening.

In the last ten years, we have seen a very interesting thing take place. Newborn babies no longer have the parental fear developing in them that they might have infantile paralysis. With the development of the Salk Vaccine, we have erased one of the great fears of their parents' world. The parents of the new baby no longer have this fear. They know that their child, inoculated at the right time, will never have this disease. Fear has been taken from the parent; therefore, it is not indoctrinated into the child. The child's mind always absorbs both the fears and the faiths of the parents' minds.

You and I were conditioned during the first eight years, given our basic premises of life and, in general, we have not varied too much from them since that age. The child takes on the attitudes, the fears, and the faith of his parents. Here we are as adults, and we have fears. Every person has certain basic fears. I do not know what yours are.

In thinking of my talk this morning, I analyzed myself and found some fears. These are quite different from the fears of 10 years ago, 20 years ago, or 30 years ago. When I first came to New York in 1946, the question in my mind was, "Can I succeed?" I have no more fear of that; it is gone. It ended after the second year, when I began to see the Church paying its own way. I then released that fear. I am not the least bit afraid now. I still have to raise $100,000 for our new building, but it does not bother me at all. I always use that statement which you will find in my book, *Treat Yourself to Life*: "He That brought me this far will take me the rest of the way." If you don't know that statement, I wish you would memorize it.

Someone may say, "Dr. Barker, you should say, "He Who." No, I wrote "He That" with deliberate intent. It was not a slip of grammar on my part at all. It was with deliberate intent because I am not discussing a person. I am defining a Principle. I am not talking of a Being in the sense of body. I am describing a Being which is becoming a Principle, which must create out of Itself, which does create out of Itself, and of which I am a part. Where I am, It is creating out of Itself, by means of me. Where you are, It is creating out of Itself by means of you.

This is why your thought has power. This is why your feelings have power. You are a mind-emotion individual. This is why the subconscious mind has the power and the authority and the law of action to do what it does. Whatever is true on the plane of the Universal is true on the plane of the particular. Whatever this Infinite Principle is doing throughout infinity and eternity, It is doing at the point where you are, in your mind.

The Mind that created the Grand Canyon is the Mind

with which you are thinking. The Mind that created the beauty of a sunset over a lake or a mountain is the Mind with which you are thinking 24 hours a day. The creativeness of life exists in every individualization of life. We are not dealing with dualism. We are not dealing with a Creative Power and what It creates. We are dealing with a Creative Power as it creates in Its creation. If you can realize this, you will have less fear. Whatever created the Grand Canyon, That is now creating in my mind, as my mind, and I am the director of my mind. I am the one working with ideas.

During the average day, my ideas would be different from yours, as yours would be different from the person's next to you. This is the principle of individualization because individualization carries with it free will. The person next to you is free to think what he wants to think. I am free to think what I want to think. You are free to think what you want to think. But, whatever I think causes something to happen because, as I think, I have a response of emotion, and the combination of thought and emotional response is the creative power of life.

I have the capacity to think, to feel, and thus create. This is not just a capacity; it is the way God works. It is not something to be theorized about on a Sunday morning or when we read a spiritual book. It is what we will be thinking tomorrow in the office. It is what we will be thinking and feeling tomorrow evening at home. It is never isolated to a day or a time, a location or a situation. You are not spiritually minded because you go to church. You are spiritually minded, period. The value of going to church is to remind you that you are. It does not make you so. It reminds you of something which, during the busy week, you may have forgotten.

I wish I could say that everyone who came here to our church would have something special in life. If I could do that, we would soon have standing room only. I can't do that because I can only tell you what you are. The more that I tell you what you are, the greater the possibility that you will forget what you aren't. When you are able to forget what you aren't, then you will no longer experience what you aren't, and you will experience what you are. This is not peculiar; it is true.

Jesus said to the blind man, "You have sight." And he had it. The blind man began dealing with what was so and ceased thinking that which was not so. Jesus spoke to another man, "Arise and walk." The man began thinking in a new direction, and he arose and walked because he had ceased to think in the old direction of "I can't" and "I never will."

The more that I remind myself of what I am spiritually, the more I will cease to be what I am not. The more that you remind yourself of what you are spiritually, the more you will cease being what you are not. You can only be what you are aware of being. You can only be what you believe yourself to be. Some of our writers call this the "self-image." I am that which I know myself to be. And I can always change what I know myself to be.

A sentence from the mind of Jesus changed a man from knowing himself as blind to knowing himself as sighted. With another sentence, this great Teacher caused a man to know himself as a walking man, and he stopped knowing himself as a paralyzed man. His new concept of himself made him the new concept in action.

When you are afraid, you are in the tentacles of the fear. As you begin to understand why you are afraid, you cease to be afraid. As a result, you are set free from the fear. Fear is ignorance; and understanding, which is its opposite, is knowledge. We are seeking the truth because it frees us from the untruth. We are seeking to know that which really is, in order to be free of that which is not.

Many years ago, while listening to a profound teacher, after the first five minutes I settled down to daydreaming because, to my mind, he was speaking utter rubbish. His discourse that particular time was how to understand the "is-notness" of life. After the first five minutes, I gave up. He continued on for an hour, but I wasn't with him. By that time I was mentally off on a trip somewhere, enjoying situations, events, and people. I still sat in the seat. I am sure I put something in the collection plate when it was passed, but he lost me in the first five minutes. I hope I haven't lost you. Now, I see exactly what the man was talking about. I couldn't then. It was all above my head because in those days I wanted God as Love. I didn't want God as Intelligence; I wanted God as Love. I wanted a God that was dear, a God that was sweet, and a God that loved people. I wanted a God that felt terrible when I felt terrible. I wanted a God that would weep with me and be afraid with me. I don't want this anymore because I know there isn't any such a God.

There is a Creative Principle in life that we have called God, and It is God. It is Impersonality, and yet I know that It is personal to me. It is a Mind, and It thinks as my mind. It is a Right Action, and this Right Action is available to me to be my action. The more that I affirm this to myself and the more that I can accept myself as being this, the less fear I shall have.

The Bible is a textbook on erasing fear. It starts with Abraham, Isaac, and Jacob down through Joseph and Moses, to the people of Israel, to the wilderness, to the occupation of the Promised Land, through the monarchies, until the destruction of Jerusalem in A.D. 70; then the strife and the turmoil thereafter portrayed so greatly by the rise of the prophets. All of them said in one way or another, "Fear not. Be not afraid." Yet the people went right on being afraid. My talk this morning may only erase a small amount of fear in us. If that is all it does, it has done much. It has accomplished a vital mission.

The stories in both the Old and the New Testaments—whether confirmed by history or whether they remain in the shadows of doubt (it makes no difference), say one thing to my mind: There is a way of meeting fear. Why don't you find it? There is a way of solving your problem. Why don't you find it?

When I read the spiritual writings of antiquity or of modern times, because revelation is continuous, I always think, "This applies to me, right now, this month. The historical record is fascinating, but it applies to me this day." I think, "If I am afraid, what am I going to do about it? Where can I find understanding that will release this fear?"

When I counsel anyone about a physical problem and I see their fear of it, I know it is a fear of the unknown. I often tell the person that before I counsel him again, he must have a medical check-up. Nine out of ten phone me and say that the doctor has found nothing wrong. Therefore, they do not need to see me again. The evidence of that which was true caused them to cease being afraid of that which was not true. The medical doctor says, "Your blood pressure is normal, your heart is normal, your well-being is normal." Then they always add, "For your age, you are in good condition." Isn't that awful?

The truth revealed is the untruth negated. Nine out of ten people, the minute a voice of authority says to them, "Your health is normal," never again think of the problem they had in their minds when they entered his office. They went to the doctor; their minds were sure of what they had. When they left the office floating on wings, they never went back to the problem. Mentally, they left it in the doctor's office. "The thing I was sure I had, I now know I didn't have." Just the flash of understanding that an authority can give clears the individual, and he is set free.

If I have a fear, what do I need to understand in order not to have it? If I have a problem, what do I need to think in order not to have it? I put this at the mental-emotional level because most people with a problem have exhausted the what-to-do level. Every Practitioner knows that one of the most familiar terms that comes across the desk is, "I have done everything, but the problem remains." Ask the person, "What have you done?" He enumerates everything at the physical-material level. These are intelligent steps to take, and I am glad he has taken them. But now he has come to the counselor, whether it be the clergyman, the Practitioner, the psychologist, or the psychiatrist, to find something in the world of thinking and feeling to be done. This is where the Practitioner does his work.

My first teacher ingrained into my consciousness a statement, "There is not something to do, there is something to be thought." If you burn your finger on the stove through carelessness and rush to the medicine chest, while you are rushing, do some thinking. There is nothing wrong with going to the medicine chest to put some ointment on the finger. It is what you think as you are going that's important. "There is not something to be done; there is only something to be thought," to be known, to be activated in the mind, to be clarified in thought.

Jesus healed the centurion's servant at a distance. I am sure the people around Jesus said that he should go and see him. But Jesus knew that it was not the movement of his body from one place to another that would heal. It was what Jesus thought, felt, and knew at the point where he was that cleared the illness in the centurion's servant at a distance away. What is thought and known at any point is thought and known at every point.

If I am afraid, then I am dealing with misunderstanding. If I have a serious problem, I am dealing with misunderstanding. If I seek, I shall find, the Bible says. If I knock at the door, it shall be opened—when I seek not at the level of what-to-do, but at the level of what-to-know. The truth known is the untruth set free. What is it that I need to know? I need to know that I am not the fear; I am its opposite. I am not the problem; I am its solution.

If the men in whom Jesus revealed sight had been really blind, the sight would have not been there, but the sight was there all the time. It was waiting for someone to know it. In you is the opposite of your problem, waiting for you to know it. In you is the opposite of your fear, waiting for you to know it. Just say, "Whatever is the opposite of this—and name it—I now am this; therefore, I am not that which I was."

The fear-ridden mind walks into the doctor's office, and a peace-saturated mind walks out. A change of knowing is all that happened. Certainly the doctor examined the body, but the doctor spoke the truth and dispelled the untruth in the person's mind. Jesus said to the man, "Blessed are your eyes for you see." And the untruth, "I shall not see and I cannot see," was dispelled.

You may say, "Dr. Barker, you make it sound so simple." I do because it is that simple. "Well, what about God?" God is the whole thing. God is the knowing in you. "What about the God of the ages?" I don't know. I only know the God that is. "Do you mean to say, Dr. Barker, that anyone can do this?" I certainly do. Whether you will or not, I have no way of knowing, but I think you will.

Here is my fear, and I name it. I am not afraid to name it. Never be afraid to name your fear. What is its opposite? The opposite of insecurity is security. I can understand security. I can think security until I am security. When I am security, I am no longer insecurity. Perhaps I am lonely and afraid of being alone all the time. What is the opposite? I am people and, as I realize that I am people, I become a fit instrument to function with people and people start functioning with me. Suddenly, the opposite is gone. Where there was ignorance, I now have knowledge, the knowing-ness. Where there was the "I can't," I now have the "I can." All I have done was to do the only thing that could be done. I have known what I wanted to experience, and it is done unto me according to my belief.

Never say that you will never again be afraid. That is stupid; you will be. I wouldn't dare say that never again shall I be afraid because I am sure I will someday. I can say that every year I am less afraid because I sense that anything that causes fear can be understood and, when it is understood, the fear goes. Thank God, we are people who can understand.

Closing Treatment

I believe in God, the Living Spirit Almighty, not as person, but as Principle. I believe in One Self-Existent Creative Cause, in you and in myself, in us, through us, as us. We leave this Church in the certainty that we are the Mind and Spirit of God in action. We are equal to every situation. Therefore, all is well. Amen.

CHAPTER 12

ARE YOU AGING, OR ARE YOU MATURING?

AS YOU probably are aware, a number of years ago the psychiatrists and medical doctors began a new field of research. They called it geriatrics. Technically, it is the psychology of the aging process. They did this because of the very rapid change that had taken place on the subject of aging in previous decades. You must realize that to be an elderly person in today's world isn't really very pleasant. This is the world's opinion. I am not an authority in the field of geriatrics. I am an observer of it.

We have unfortunately discredited the aging process. We have made growing old something not very nice and to be avoided under all conditions. Everyone is supposed to maintain a physical appearance of about the age of 20.

I have often told our students that the last time I tried to buy swimming trunks I discovered they had not designed any male swimming trunks for anyone over 20 years of age. They allow for very few variations. So, it made me quite self-conscious to appear on the beach in that which was available!

Our whole thinking about age has changed. Up until the first world war, perhaps until the second, the aging process was respected, was expected, and we were geared to it. This has all changed. It is a subject to be avoided at all costs. We are, on every hand, made conscious of our age if we are past 30. And, for those of you who are under 30, you had better start doing some thinking. The first premise of the psychological field in geriatrics is that you and I start to age the day we are born. Furthermore, our last 10 years of life manifest the emotional patterns we created in the first 10 years. That is why you and I have noticed that people, as they grow old, quite often become very dictatorial. They weren't this way in their twenties, thirties, or forties, but as time moves on, the tantrums and demands of childhood begin to repeat their patterns.

What do we in our philosophy say about all this? Our entire Science is based upon the premise that you can operate your own mind and your own emotions. You need be a part of the collective mind and emotion only to the extent that you choose to be. As an individual, meaning an independent mental-emotional entity, you can, if you want to, change any pattern at any time.

Here is where our teaching differs greatly from the academic psychological field, because they would not make that statement. They are not attempting to understand spiritual values. They do not look upon the individual mind as a spiritual potential, having within itself capacities, potentials, and possibilities. These can be brought to the surface when understood by the individual and then can be used by the individual. The mind you will use at 90 is the mind you are using right now. Mind doesn't change. The body will change. If you are only 15 years of age today, the mind you will use at the age of 90 is the mind you are using right now. At the age of 90, your mind will have a great deal more information than it had at 15. It will have had a great deal of experience that it did not have at 15. It may even have serious warping, called neurotic states, which it did not have at 15, but it is the same mind, and mind is always amenable to change. Mind is never fixed unless you have arranged it to be fixed. Mind is never set in its ways unless you have set it in its ways, meaning you have formed patterns in the subconscious mind that determine the operation of mind.

The greatest key to maturing is the word *flexibility* and the acceptance of change. The key to aging is inflexibility and not wanting to change.

One of our speakers some years ago developed as his theme this statement, "I mature in the pattern of youth." I like that. "I mature in the pattern of youth." This doesn't mean you are not going to mature. The people who say, "I will never grow old," are ridiculous. They make themselves ridiculous because such a statement is an impossible one.

Things have been changing since the day you were born. They are going to continue to change long after you have gone on to the next plane of life. You may say, "Yes, but the changes are unpleasant." This is one of the signs of the aging process—not the maturing process, the aging process. Crusty, elderly people are always wishing they could turn back the calendar and have things as they used to be. Now, when you were growing up, however many years ago it was, you heard the same cliches we hear today. Young people were going to the ways of the Devil. This was true probably 5,000 years ago. In those days they had not yet invented the Devil. Actually, the Devil in Judeo-Christian thought was developed during the Babylonian captivity, around B.C. 600. We don't believe in him anyway.

For some people, current situations have always been wrong. When you hear people talking this way today, at any age level, you realize that you have a mind that has deserted its own creativeness. There is a Creative Mind in your mind. When this is known and activated, you flow with life. You move with the current of the NOW. You do not resist that which is obvious. You do not try to hide from what is taking place. For what is taking place is nothing but the repetition of old, old patterns. There have been wars and rumors of wars since the year One, according to modern historians. There has been disease since the year One. There has been death since the year One. There have been miserable people since the year One. Because we are in a population explosion, there may be more miserable people now than ever before, but that is only due to the population explosion. There were people who lived a calm, quiet life of very hard work on isolated farms who also developed neurotic states. Then there were people in the busy urban areas who didn't, because this has nothing to do with location. It has nothing to do with the "times" in which we function. It has to do with how we have set down our patterns in our own subconscious mind.

I am constantly talking with people who see nothing but trouble around them and nothing but trouble ahead of them. I ask, "What are you going to do about it?" Repeating all those negatives to me doesn't change anything. Anyone who does counseling work hears them all the time. If I believed everything everyone told me in my counseling work, I would have been a serious neurotic 20 years ago.

What about these people who are dissatisfied with life? They would be dissatisfied with life if they had been born 50 years earlier or if they had been born 50 years later. They are the way they are because of the way they have unconsciously allowed themselves to become. You and I are trying to break some of these patterns. We do not want to end up as bitter, seemingly disillusioned, fairly sick, neurotic people. At least I don't. And I don't think you do either.

Do I have some suggestions to make? I most certainly do. I named two of them: flexibility and the capacity to accept change as normal. The third, you have to be interested in life to be alive. Never lose interest in being alive. Next, the aged withdraw from life; the mature continue to function in the mainstream of life. Observe some of the people you know, and you will see this very clearly. For those who are withdrawing, their circle of activity is getting smaller and smaller. But those who are maintaining and expanding their activities have a vital interest in life. I often wonder why people's minds go sour when you and I exist in and are a part of the greatest, most fascinating civilization that has ever been. There is more to be known, seen, felt, and experienced today than ever before in the history of this planet. It is even piped right into your home by radio and TV. You don't have to go out for it as much as you would have 50 years ago. It delivers itself to you for a few pennies of electric current. This present universe is exciting to those who can see it as being exciting. Or, this present universe is in terrible trouble for those who want to sit and contemplate nothing but negatives. One of the great things I regret is that more and more people are becoming more and more negative. I do not intend to join their ranks. I can't afford to. I want no part of it. The present situation needs people with faith and hope.

I believe that God is still in business. I believe that the universe is still the operation of Divine Intelligence, that life is still creative, and that you and I can be a part of it on the right side of experience. But to do this takes a great deal of correct mental work. I need to ask myself, "Am I maturing, or am I aging? Am I flexible, or am I inflexible? Are my little idiosyncrasies, which I have covered up all these years, beginning to show?" We have a tendency to get a little peculiar as we age, and many of our idiosyncrasies suddenly begin to show around the edges. Are you really interested in the new, fresh, and different? The need of the maturing mind is to be present in its concept and to be seeking the freshness of today. Today is the only experience you have. Yesterday ended last night, and tomorrow hasn't been born. So, all you can do is to explore the NOW. Like you, when I begin to explore the NOW, there are many things in it I don't like. But I don't have to like them because in between there are so many things I do like. In between my dislikes, there are a few apertures, a few breakthroughs into which I can find some good. I am interested in the present and future good of humanity. I am not just sitting, reading the newspapers, and listening to the news on the radio, thus implanting negatives in my subconscious mind.

The world has never been improved by pessimists. The world has never been improved by gloom. Ernest Holmes wrote, "When will we ever wake up to the fact that the world has learned enough through suffering?" I am not going to suffer for you, nor am I going to suffer with you. If I suffer, I will do an excellent job of it on my own, and I have no plans in that direction. Life is still for the living. There is love, there is life, there is intelligence, there is wisdom, there is the new, the fresh, the different, the vital, the creative, and the dynamic. If you will just put a few small holes in all of your doubts, in all of your fears, and in all of your negative assumptions, you will see these things. You will experience these things. You will keep flexible. You will keep having goals. You will keep interested in life. And, you will become aware of your condemnations. It takes neither intelligence nor virtue to complain about everything.

I think it does take intelligence and persistence to find the good and praise it. This we can do. We are equipped with a mind that can do it. I am vitally interested in being alive this year. You see, I do not want my mind to be negative. I do not want my mind to become set, to become bitter; I want to always be open to that which is on the side of greatness.

Emerson said in one of his writings that the individual grows only when he is uncomfortable. This is a very interesting observation. The individual grows in consciousness and awareness only when he is uncomfortable. The individual grows only when he is *creatively* uncomfortable. I know a great many uncomfortable people who, due to their groaning and whining, are only going to be more uncomfortable. They are not uncomfortable in a creative way.

Your experience always has been and is now an experience of awareness, an experience of consciousness, an experience that is taking place in your mind and your emotions. Here is the place where you can determine direction. There are many situations in the world around me that I cannot do anything about except I can change what I am thinking and feeling about them. The one point of dominion you and I have is our individual use of mind. This is our one point of total dominion when we assume it. In this mind in which you and I function there is the creativity of what we will call God, the creativity of idea, the creativity of motivation; and when we do some thinking about these, we realize that our experience is taking place in our minds and not in our bodies.

In mind, you and I are individual. We are if we want to be. We can be in control. I want to understand the spiritual creativity that is in my mind right now. I want to be flexible, to flow with change, whether I like it or not. I want to maintain a healthy interest in living. I want to explore the new and the possible. I want to mature in the pattern of youth, and that is what I want you to do, also.

CHAPTER 13

THERE IS NO OLD AGE

"The problem of old age cannot be solved by beauty salons and barber shops. It can only be solved in your mind."

Opening Remarks

WE ARE of one mind in one place and of one accord. That is a familiar statement of Scripture—to be in one place, of one mind, of one accord. When we are in one place and of one mind and of one accord, something unusual happens. In the Book of Acts, second chapter, it tells of Pentecost, an unusual experience dealing with phenomena. We expect here this morning the phenomena of changed minds, changed conditions, and changed situations.

The Bible has taught me that any person at any time can change the events and the course of his life. In the tradition of both Judaism and Christianity, this has been emphasized over and over again. The world Scriptures have said this same thing in one way or another. When an individual changes on the inside, he changes on the outside. Until he changes on the inside, there cannot be a change on the outside of any value.

Modern society is trying to change us on the outside. We are trying to live successfully on the outside of life. Yet, every great spiritual teacher has stated that the inside of life is the only real life. "As a man thinketh in his heart, so is he." Jesus said, "It is done unto you according to your belief." It is the inside of man that is important, not the outside.

We are in the midst of a predicament as old as time itself. Shall I do that which the inside, the Spirit, tells me to do? The inside versus the outside. Intuition versus intellect. The Spirit versus the world. Is there a solution? When we are at our peak, at our finest, at our highest, and at our best, we always work from the inside. When we are only one to accomplish, out to gain, acquire, struggle, then we are working from the outside level, and we are not at our best. Every great idea that has ever been thought was thought by a man or a woman thinking from the inside, believing in Something on the inside. Every progress, every adventure, everything new has come to us, because someone on the inside said, "Let us change the outside."

Jesus came, as had the prophets before him, saying, "Change yourselves if you want a changed world." The people listened, they were impressed, and they did nothing about it. So, the time came when it was necessary for Jesus to leave human sight. He spent one or three years according to historians, teaching an inside way of life. A few heard; probably his own disciples did not understand him until after his death, probably they could not grasp the idea, but once he was gone, they grasped the idea that the inside is the real creative process.

In Religious Science, we call this inside by the term *consciousness* or *awareness*, the fact that you know who you are, and that you know that you are. This is consciousness. This is the inside. When the inside is controlled, the outside is controlled. When the inside is inspired, the outside is healthy, vital, creative. When the inside is not inspired, when vision has dimmed within, then we have a lethargic individual. Such a person only does what needs to be done because it needs to be done.

We are surrounded by people doing what needs to be done only because it needs to be done. These people work in offices, factories, in every department of life. They do things because they need to be done, not because they want to do them. Because it has to be done, it is done. This is drabness and frustration. This is everything that goes against the grain of the Spirit.

The great spiritual teachers didn't do things they didn't want to do. They never conformed. Each one was a nonconformist. They did not agree with the world around them. They did not agree with the society in which they lived. They did not agree with the times in which they were born. They made no attempt to agree. Each one of them, from the Prophet Amos straight down through Jesus, said that the inside life is the only life. If you want to live on the outside, fine, but then you must take what goes with the outside. The outside of life is one of headache, strain, and struggle. It is the life of many things but few ideas.

We are interested in a spiritually easier way. Jesus said that there was one. A yoke that was easy and a burden that was light. This is the way of the inside, the way of consciousness. It is so easy once you find it. I invite you to relax and find it by thinking with me.

The Treatment

I relax. I let go of the tensions of the past week, I let go of the tensions of that which still needs to be done. I relax. In my relaxation, I realize that the Spirit of God is within me. This Spirit within me is kindly. It is warm. It is intelligent. It is loving. It is wise. It is harmonious. I let the inward order and the inward harmony now take over my mind. I let the inward intelligence and the inward peace take over my consciousness. I forget offices, apartments, houses, things to do, places to go, and people to meet. I forget all this. "The Spirit of God hath made me, and the breath of the Almighty hath given my life" (Job 33:4). Life is the understanding of myself as Spirit. In me now is the Spirit, the Wisdom of the Almighty. The Divine Breath, the activity of intelligence, makes me realize that I am not created to strain or struggle. I am created to be at peace with myself and with my fellow man. I am created to be alive, healthy, and vital. I am created to be spirit, to be life, to be love. This is my purpose. I now release the past that would claim my attention. I say praise God that Good is everywhere, praise God for love we all may share, for life that thrills in you and me, praise God for truth that sets us free.

Sermon

WHILE TALKING this morning on the subject, "There Is No Old Age," I am reminded of a statement Dr. Frederick Bailes makes in his book, *Your Mind Can Heal You*. Without a doubt it is the finest single book we have on the subject of spiritual healing in our entire field of thought. He writes, "There are no incurable diseases; there are only incurable people," I say, "There is no old age, there are just people who are expecting it." The great thing that

Dr. Quimby, the founder of this system discovered, later Mrs. Eddy amplified, and afterwards Dr. Holmes clarified, was that you either live by the world thought or you don't. If you are going to practice Religious Science, you cannot live according to world opinion.

The world sells you from the day you are born the idea that you are going to get old. I know the medical causation of the aging process. I know psychological causation. It still comes down to one fact. Are you going to believe what the world tells you? Are you going to believe what the Spirit within tells you? This is the entire answer to the old-age question. I know people at 50 as old in their attitudes as people at 85. I know people at 85 that are younger than I am in their attitudes, interests, and creativity.

Old age is not a calendar idea. Old age is what you honestly believe about old age. It is not what the medical field defines. It is not what the psychologist defines. In the Bible we read about the veneration of old age. Bible people liked to live long, and Bible people liked to live well. The prophets of the Bible venerated old age. They believed in the wisdom and maturity of old age. Today's world doesn't. It believes that only the young are bright. This false concept is forced upon us by the world opinion.

Any person over 50 years of age is practically unemployable in modern society. The reason I know that is because an authority in the field of employment talked with me one day and told me that at my age I was unemployable if I ever wanted to leave the ministry. Luckily, I didn't want to leave the ministry. I asked, "Couldn't I sell things, because I would be good at that?" This person said that they don't even hire salesmen at my age if they can help it. So, this church is stuck with me now; I can't get another job.

The world is shouting age at everyone. We insure children the day that they are born, to take care of their old age. There is nothing wrong with insurance; that is not what I am talking about. I am talking about the world thought conditioning. Our entire attitude towards old age is that there is something indecent about it. It is almost immoral to be too old. Did you know it? That is what the world says. It is almost immoral to be too old. It isn't quite nice. This is what people are thinking. I am only uncovering and exposing a cancer of society, instead of a cancer of the body.

I intend to mature, but I do not intend to have old age. I intend to live to my last breath, but to live victoriously, actively, dynamically, and happily. You may say that when I'm 75, I won't feel the way I do now. I don't know whether I will or whether I won't, but I do know I will have more sense. I probably won't want to do half the things I want to do now. Looking back 30 years in my own life, I don't want to do things today I did 30 years ago. I have no interest in them. I see people 30 years younger doing them all the time, and I think this is great. I am glad I did what I did. I am delighted with every sin I ever committed. I am thoroughly pleased that I did everything I did. I think it would be dreadful to go to my grave and not have had all this experience. You and I are greater because of our mistakes, and that is all the word *sin* means. Average people don't sin. They are either afraid of taking the chance, or the desire has been scared out of them by the theologians. At the age of 70, they look back on a blameless life, and it is terrible, just dreadful!

I don't want to do what I did 30 years ago. Twenty-five years from now I won't want to do many things I am doing today. This is a normal change. This is maturing. This is growing up. We have the false standard that anyone over 21 years of age is grown up and anyone under 21 is not. The world sets this line. I am an adult because I am over 21. There are more immature people running around over 21 than we could ever count. We have many people over 21 acting childish and not childlike.

Everyone is old at the level at which he is functioning. We say, "There is a five-year-old," when we speak of a child. "This is a 16-year-old," when we speak of a teen-ager. Suddenly at the age of 21 he becomes the adult. Next, the world forces on us the belief that you have to get everything done between 21 and 40. Years ago we had a bestselling book, *Life Begins at Forty*, and it helped a great deal. It woke up a great many people.

You are as young as your inspiration, and you are as old as your lack of it. That is the key to the living process. I call it the living process, not the aging process, because the term *aging* indicates gradual deterioration, and it isn't that at all. The living process is dependent upon spiritual inspiration. I believe all inspiration to be spiritual. It is dependent upon a desire to express, to see, to grasp, to adventure. And, there are people 21 years of age who have already lost this.

As long as you are inspired and interested in the new, you are in a constant circulation of new activities. You will stay youthful; you will stay ageless. You are freed from that terrible word *age* as long as you have inspiration and adventure. But the whole world thought is lined up against you, if you believe this. What can you do to be inspired and to be adventurous? Break every old pattern, rut, and habit you have gradually, one by one. Watch out for the ruts in your life. Watch out for routines. They are too easy to maintain because you have done them repeatedly and always the same way.

I know a man who spent a great deal of money going to Europe to study with a great mystic. It is not important who the teacher was. This man went to the mystic and asked, "What is the first thing I should do to start on the spiritual pathway?" The mystic said, "Reverse everything you normally do." When my friend asked him what he meant, the mystic said, "When you get up tomorrow morning, get out of the other side of the bed. Put the other foot down first. Whatever you do in getting dressed for the day, use the other hand. If you always brush your teeth with the right hand, use your left. If you always comb your hair with your right hand, comb it with the left. Change everything." Much annoyed, my friend told him that he had come for spiritual instruction. The mystic answered, "You are getting it." This was a great teacher. It took my friend several months to get out of the routines that he now saw were engulfing him. Whether this teacher's method was right or wrong is not the question. It gives us food for thought.

Can the aging process in the body be stopped? Yes, it can. I have recently made a study of a book called *Man's Presumptuous Brain*, written by a psychiatrist of excellent repute, A. T. W. Simeons, M.D., an authority in the field of psychosomatic medicine in Europe for many years. He heads a large psychosomatic department in a hospital in Rome, Italy. There is not one particular place in the book where he states the point I am making, but this is what I got from his book. Dr. Simeons implies that the reason the body ages is tension, and the way to prevent the body from aging is relaxation. I would say relaxation plus inspiration. Anything you can do to break a rut, anything you can do to lessen tension, adds to the length of your life. Dr. Simeons, after studying thousands of patients with hardening of the arteries, is absolutely convinced that the disease has nothing to do with cholesterol. It has to do with one thing only—tension.

The tension habit pattern starts within the week after you are born. It is like people who are nervous. A patient said to me the other day that he was nervous. I answered, "Who isn't? It is normal; that is what nerves are for. If you weren't nervous, you would be a totally inhuman being. You would be a walking statue." Next he said he got jittery over things. I answered, "Who doesn't? You don't need a tranquilizer; you need God. You need a spiritual understanding of this present arena of life."

If the world is making me tense, it is because I let it. If the world is telling me I'm old, it is because I believe it. If the world is constantly pressing upon me age, age, age, it is because I let it.

We are basically nothing but consciousness. We are mind and emotion using body. And, consciousness does not have a time schedule. The body may—I'm sure it does. But, your mind and your emotions, your capacity of awareness, your ability to think and to feel are not in a time reference. They are in a "now" reference. There is no time at the level of thought and feeling. You do not age at the level of thought and feeling. You can be a brilliant thinker and have great emotion at 90. I mean a well-disciplined emotion, a healthy, outgoing emotion. Your body may not have the resiliency it once did, but taking this factor of tension into account, your body can have greater resiliency, greater flexibility, if you take certain clear stands in consciousness.

My friend who went to Paris to study with the mystic makes me question how to break the ruts I'm in. Watch the ruts in the daily events of your life. You get up at the same time. You don't have to. You go to bed at the same time. You don't have to. You eat the same breakfast. You usually have the same lunch; you only vary what goes in between two pieces of bread. To a great extent, you eat about the same foods seven nights a week. When did you, yourself, invent a new dish to eat? When was the last time you went to a restaurant you have never been to before?

Some years ago, we had a minister on our staff, Mrs. Ella Pomeroy, who lived into her nineties. She decided that she was not going to allow the aging process to overtake her. At the age of 60, she realized that she had never learned to swim. She decided she would, and took swimming lessons. She perfected her swimming and decided it was time to learn to dive and took diving lessons. She swam and dived right up into her eighties, and she didn't start until she was 60 years old.

In Mrs. Pomeroy's church in Brooklyn, she had ten elderly ladies who looked elderly, thought elderly, and reacted elderly. She said to them, "I'm going to start breaking up some of your old patterns. Will you go with me to various moderate-priced restaurants one day a week?" She made a study of the restaurants of New York City and, of course, discovered that we have the greatest variety there is in the world. We have a far greater variety than there is in any large city in the world, more than in London, Paris, Rome, Vienna, and so on. She took these ladies once a week to foreign restaurants they had never known before, and they ate food they had never eaten before. Here was someone who had a new idea.

Most of us, living in the area of New York City where there are at least 20,000 restaurants, almost always eat in the same few ones. We call them "our favorites." Even the Horn and Hardart people have their favorite Horn and Hardart's. Yes, they have their favorite one—the vegetables are fresher at that one. I have heard about the fresh vegetables at Horn and Hardart's for 20 years and, so far, I have successfully avoided them. I have eaten their apple pie; that is great. The Horn and Hardart people have their favorite Horn and Hardart's, the Schrafft's people have their favorite Schrafft's, the Stouffer's people have their favorite Stouffer's. If you eat at a hotel, you usually go to the one you have always gone to. You would think you were living in a town of 50,000 people where there are only three good restaurants.

I am throwing out suggestions. Break your ruts. You don't need to change the way you get out of bed, but you do need to change your other ruts. Anything that is the same old pattern, watch it and break it. If you always shop in one store, change it. Once in a while, shop somewhere else. If you know the higher echelon of marketing these days, all the stores get the same thing from the same places and put their own labels on them. Don't be kidded by your pet store. If you are a Macy-ite, there is something good at Gimbel's. If you are a Gimbel-ite, try Bloomingdale's. If you are a Bloomindale-ite, try Stern's. If you are a Stern-ite, try something in Brooklyn. You go to the same supermarket, the same gas station, the same this, the same that, and pretty soon you don't have to think.

One night a week you have a hamburger, the next night you have ham, the next night you have chicken, the next night you have beef, and on your night out, you usually go to your favorite restaurant where you have gone for 30 years and sit at the same table and talk with the same waitress and eat the same items on the menu. Occasionally, you change the ham from Tuesday to Thursday, but that's about the most change you make.

The world is exploding with new ideas, and we sit in the routine, the rut, and the aging process. This is how you age cheese, beer, and whiskey. You leave it alone. You don't touch it for years. I know people who haven't touched or changed anything in their lives for years, and they look like old cheese, old beer, and old whiskey. The Bible says, "Behold I make all things new" (Revelation 21:5). That is what the Good Book says.

Every savior upset the people to whom he talked. He said to the people, "If you are going to stay in the routine of your present ways, my message has no value." If you are going to stay the way you are, then you don't need spiritual help or inspiration. Once in a while the great teachers through history found a few people willing to change. Wherever they found people willing to change, then a change in history took place.

Routine and tensions: What makes you tense, and what can you do about it? You can always do something about it. If things disturb you, you can do something about them. If you can't make changes at the material level, then make them at the mental-emotional level. Quietly say to yourself, "Who is going to win? The situation that makes me tense, or am I going to win? The problem upsets me. It disturbs me. It keeps me awake nights. It builds up my blood pressure. It causes hardening of my arteries. It does all this to me. Do I want these negative effects? Is my argument with the owner of my apartment house worth it? Is the argument going on in the office worth it? Is the argument going on in the neighborhood worth it?"

Say to yourself: "Within me is a Divine Center, something of the Spirit. It is undisturbed, even though I may be disturbed." As you calm down and think of your own spiritual center, you relax. I have watched this take place in my consultations with troubled people. They come into my office and sit down tense. They talk, and I relax and listen. Soon, I watch them shift in the chair, their shoulders go down, their neck straightens out, their bodies become less stiff, even their fingers relax. I know a healing has taken place that had nothing to do with me. They talked themselves into relaxation without knowing they did it. They relaxed.

Your body is the temple of the Living God. This is correct spiritual thinking. It is not made for tension. If tension does what Dr. Simeons and other authorities say it does, sit down once in a while alone and relax. Take five minutes and stop worrying. Just five minutes! For five minutes, stop worrying about anything. You can go right back to worrying when you get through. For five minutes don't worry about your bank account. Stop fussing over what she said, he said, they did, and we did. Stop contemplating the past. For five minutes, think about yourself as a spiritual possibility. You are more loving than you think you are. You probably have not made half the mistakes that you think you have.

For five minutes, in calmness, in quiet, contemplate yourself from the highest point of view. Emerson wrote, "Prayer is the contemplation of life from the highest point of view." The rest of the time, we are contemplating it from lower levels. Contemplate yourself from the highest point of view. For a moment, let tension be gone.

What to do about old age? Don't do anything about it. Do you fight it? No. Just never expect it. The world thought has trained us to expect disease. In Religious Science, in this new thought of God, of man, of life, we minimize disease. There is less disease in our congregation than there is in any church congregation in the city of New York. We have very few sick people compared to the number who go through our doors in the course of a week. Why? We don't believe it is necessary to be sick. God didn't make a sick man. God didn't create you to deteriorate. God made you to glorify life. You will not grow old. You will mature. You are going to change, but you are not on a road of deterioration. God never made such a pathway. You are on the pathway of the Lord.

Watch your ruts, watch your tensions. Don't let the world tell you about old age. Don't study old age. Change events and people in your life regularly. Bring new people into your life. Too often I get the plaintive question, "Where can I meet new people, Dr. Barker?" When I listen to the tone of voice, I answer, "You can't." People don't like whiners. If you did sit down with someone for 15 minutes, what would you talk about that was interesting? People are not interested in what you did 20 years ago, not the least bit interested. What can you talk about now that someone will find interesting?

"Behold I make all things new." There is always a new way when you want a new way. There is a great advantage in being old and crotchety. You will have to give up that advantage. The older you get, the nastier you can be and get away with it. The older you get, the meaner you can be and get away with it. Not all people grow old graciously. Some do, but they are in the minority. Watch your tempers, watch your criticisms, break your ruts, watch your tensions. Love God, and believe in your own soul, and you will mature in the pattern of youth.

The Benediction

I shall close this service by doing some very serious thinking with you. I shall follow Emerson's injunction that prayer is the contemplation of life from the highest point of view. I ask you to think of yourself in this way:

I am created and recreated by the Mind and Heart of God at every instant. I am spirit. I am life. I am timeless, ageless, birthless, deathless. I am on an eternal pathway led, governed, and controlled by the Spirit. I am youthful, creative, dynamic. I am not afraid of my own body. I am not afraid of changes in my body. I am not afraid. I am a Spirit. I am Life. The Power that created me out of Itself indwells me. This Power is timeless, ageless. God doesn't know my age and isn't interested in it. I am the eternal action of the Eternal Mind of God, in health, vitality, and energy, here and now. I decree this. I am younger than I think I am. Amen.

CHAPTER 14

MAN WITHOUT LIMITATION

"Hast thou not known, has thou not heard, that the everlasting God, the Lord, the Creator of the ends of the earth, fainteth not, neither is weary? There is no searching of his understanding.

"He giveth power to the faint; and to them that have no might he increaseth strength.

"Even the youths shall faint and be weary, and the young men shall utterly fall.

"But they that wait upon the Lord shall renew their strength; they shall mount up with wings as eagles; they shall run, and not be weary; and they shall walk, and not faint."

(Isaiah 40:28–31)

SOME YEARS AGO there appeared a book that caused a sensation. It was *The Unobstructed Universe*. It had a tremendous sale, which was good, because it awakened people to the fact that the universe is not what it appears to be. Religions through the ages have been trying to tell us that. And, in the last 50 years, our experts in physics have been telling us that it is not all that it appears to be.

We are in an unobstructive universe. We are not only in an unobstructed universe, but we are also unobstructed people who are temporarily obstructed by the projections of our own minds. I am absolutely convinced that I exist in a universe that is the operation of my mind. Most people believe that the manifest universe is something that they must work against in order to achieve success. I do not believe that. I believe that the present universe is as easy to manipulate as my personal affairs are. I can walk out of church this morning and decide where I want to eat, what street I might like to walk on, and what I want to do the rest of this day. I am in charge of my personal affairs. Seemingly, there are conditions over which I do not have domination. But, the thing that I believe controls me, is something I am unconsciously letting control me, because I do not understand it.

The Universe is an unlimited system, and there is no reason why you, as an individual, are not an unlimited individual. You may say, "The great spiritual minds have been able to do phenomena that I cannot do." Usually, you pick out the exaggerated reports we have of great spiritual personalities and say, "These people could do it, but I can't." Unconsciously, you believe that these people have a special quality that you do not have.

One of the basic teachings of the Science of Mind is that the Universe, by its very nature, can never play favorites. The Universe must be an impartial expression of an all-knowing Intelligence. By its very unity and cohesiveness it indicates that it gives of itself to all. As a Universe it never restricts anyone. Thus, all limitation is self-limitation.

The things that prevent me from doing what I want to do are the creations of my own subjective mind. As they are the creations of my own subjective mind, they can be dissolved, dissipated, and finished by my own subjective mind because they are only in my area of perception and experience because I believe they are there. If I could arrive at a point of not knowing that they are there, it is possible that they would not be there. The world calls that very foolish talk, but it is the entire basis of what we are teaching. It is the basis of all spiritual instruction, whether you study it in the teachings of Moses, Jesus, Buddha, Mohammed, or any of the other world teachers.

The essence of all religion is that we are not what we ought to be, but we can be it. But, the way in which we become greater is an interior one in the operation of our own minds. That is why every spiritual system made its followers seek within themselves. They have implied that the manifest Universe fools you, and people fool you, as long as you believe that the Universe and people have power over you. Jesus said, "Judge not by appearances, but judge righteous judgment." Yet, on a Sunday, you look out of your window and see rain and decide whether or not to go to church. That is a good example.

The Universe is not what it seems to be materially. It is the result of cosmic Intelligence, operating through flexible substance under Law, producing an infinite panorama of creative things. This is the real Universe I am in, whether I call it New York City, Town Hall, or my apartment or office. The place where I live is the atmosphere in the universal cosmic Order, where I function with ease. My office is the atmosphere in the universal panorama of cosmic Intelligence, where I operate with efficiency. My church is the atmosphere in the universal creative Mind, where I become aware of that Mind. It is all one thing. If the Universe is that, and it is, it explains why Jesus said Heaven was on earth, and the Heaven was where you were.

Jesus knew that everyone was waiting to get somewhere, instead of being something now. Everyone wants to become something, instead of being it. We do not realize that the thing we want to become, we already are. We would have to be it or we could not want to become it. The thing you want to be is the thing you are. If you would stop becoming and start being, you would have it.

A newcomer to this Science will say that this is a pleasant play on words, but what on earth is this all about? I am merely saying what Jesus said, what Moses said, what Paul said, and what every spiritual teacher has said in his own language and time. Never once did Jesus say that he was going to be the Son of God. He announced that he was. Since his time, we have always been going to become the Sons of God, and we have not accomplished it yet.

Very few people have the courage to announce, "I am the expression of God." Rather, we look for a technique, a procedure, a delaying action. We are always going to become a Son of God. We think that perhaps the easiest way to become It is to die in the arms of the church, and then we are sure to be all right. Of course, that is no assurance at all. I am anxious to get to the next plane to see some of those people who are so sure of everything. I want to watch them as they come in and ask, "Where is my harp?" It is easier to be virtuous after death, just as it is much easier to be virtuous after age 70.

You are unlimited right now. But, as long as your full attention is on why you cannot be successful, you cannot be successful. The problem-ridden mind is the static mind that is subjectively content in the problems. The problem-ridden mind has gone stale; it is the mind that says, "I will endure." Such people like to quote, "He that endureth to the end shall be saved" (Matthew 10:22). In other words, if I put up with all the negatives in my life and manage to live into my seventies, I will receive a crown of glory. That is not at all what Jesus meant. He meant that people who endure in thinking rightly to the end of their problem, receive their demonstration. The person who says, "I am limited," is stating a false conditioning of life that he has accepted. He cannot solve his problem, because his attention is too fixed on the problem. Most people who get well become sick again, because their attention is too fixed on the problem. Most people who get well become sick again, because they never stopped being sick in their own minds. Most people who have consistent financial troubles continue to have them because they subconsciously believe them to be normal.

Jesus upset the affairs, the minds, and the hearts of a great many people. They had been going along in their unconsciously contented pathway of restriction. They had unconsciously accepted their problem as normal. Jesus declared they did not have to do this. It is no wonder they decided to be rid of him.

The people around Jesus were so busy trying to tell him why they could not be what they wanted to be that he was only able to help a few. When he was able to break through the negatives, the person changed because he stopped accepting his problem as normal. We could have a depression tomorrow, and serious right-thinking people would not be involved in it. We could have a prosperity boom tomorrow, and a seriously negative person would not improve his finances. He would still be getting his $45 a week and continue his grumbling. You can pour money on some people, and it does not stick, because their consciousness is not ready for it. If you still have that old bugaboo, read my booklet, "Money Is God In Action." It will clear you on money once and for all. Use the money treatment in it, and expect it to happen. Why can you have more money? Because money is impersonal. The money in the Manufacturers Trust Company does not care who uses it. It is waiting to be used. The person who uses it is the person who knows that he can use it.

Unlimited man. He is the greatest single potential in all of recorded history—a creative animal gone civilized, who can walk, talk, think, act, decide, feel, and sense—an individual who has evolved to a point where his mind can be trained to do anything. This same individual, instead of taking his mind, his emotions, and his capacity and using them as free agents to create a better world for himself and for his fellow men, abides in the routines of abnormal problems and says, "Look at poor me." Jesus taught that it does not have to be that way.

Jesus believed that health was God, and he demonstrated it. If Jesus for one split second had ever believed that sickness was normal, he could never have healed anyone. There has never been an effective Practitioner in Religious Science who did not first convince himself that health was absolutely normal and that sickness of any kind was nonsense. Yet, you have friends who would not believe that, no matter how many Bible quotations you gave them. You could present case histories as I have done in my book *Treat Yourself to Life* and they would merely say, "He thought those up out of his own head." But I didn't. The way you accept yourself is the way in which you experience life.

There is a Mind that knows, there is a Law that acts, there is a Spirit that gives of Itself, and I am Its individualization. It works through me, but I have been concentrating on problems. In my imagination I have built tremendous problems. I have accepted them, sat back in them, and enjoyed self-pity and the sympathy of others. It is time that I arose and went unto my Father. It is time that I finished with the husks of my problems and began to assert myself and dissolve my negatives. That is what Isaiah talked about, to run and not be weary, because you know that the Power that causes you to run is the Power that maintains you as you run.

Whatever the nature of God is, you are Its embodiment, you are Its action, you are It made visible at the point where you are. Say to yourself, "I am weary of wasting energy on the problems I accept. Within me is the Christ, the living Son of God, and I am It, and It is unconditioned and free. I now look beyond my problems to the solution. At the moment I may not see how it is going to happen, when it is going to happen, but at least I know it will happen, which is more than most people do."

Jesus said, "Follow thou me." In other words, get going. There isn't a problem in your life today if you will stop living in it, analyzing it, dissecting it, and asking why it happened, that cannot be solved. I don't know why it happened to you, but it did happen to you, so what are you going to do about it? That is the message of the great Teacher. This is the Science of Mind. Manipulate your ideas for a progressive, creative, forward movement, and cease tarrying in the comfort of your problem. We should run and not be weary; we should walk and not faint. We should rise up with youth like the eagle, and we should soar with our minds centered on God.

CHAPTER 15

YESTERDAY ENDED LAST NIGHT

Opening Remarks

"Possibility versus Probability"

WE BELIEVE in God, and we believe in man. We believe in the power of mind and the power of love. Beyond these, I don't think we have any stated opinion. We are probably the most liberal of the liberals. We are the least opinionated group of people around because we only believe in God and in you. We believe in ourselves. We believe in the Mind and the Love of God in action in the Universe.

There is a dual law of possibility and probability. Religious Science deals with possibility and seeks to disregard probability. Possibility is of the Spirit, and probability is of the human mind. Most people are limited by their belief in probability and their failure to hold fast to possibility. Here in the United States, we say that any male citizen born in this country has the possibility of becoming the President of the United States. Then instantly we conclude that under the law of probability, this little boy or that little boy will probably not be President. With that, we sign away everything. We tell young people that it is possible in an economy such as we have today for any person to accomplish almost anything, but that probably they will fall into the routine of a set job and go no further than that.

Keep with possibility, not probability. Possibility negates everything from illness and age to the whole kit and caboodle of limitations. It is too easy to say that something probably won't be true for me or for a situation or for whatsoever, instead of staying at the level of possibility. The genius of a mind like Jesus was that he stayed at the level of possibility. He did not work with the law of probability. This is why he could do the phenomenal things he did. It was not probable that he should do them, but he didn't know that. He stayed at a point of possibility. I would like this week for you and I to go back to possibility. What can you be, and why aren't you? What can I be, and why aren't I? Because it is possible for us to become what we want to be.

All things are possible. The Bible states, "With God all things are possible" (Matthew 19:26), because the Divine

Wisdom doesn't know what can't be done. The Divine Wisdom doesn't know you as a limited factor. It only knows you as a possibility. "This is my beloved Son, in whom I am well pleased" (Matthew 3:17). The Infinite Spirit does not know that you have self-conditioned yourself. Unknowingly, you have self-conditioned yourself to the level of probability. Saying "At my age, my lack of experience, or this, or that, or the other," is accepting the law of probability.

It is possible that you won't have a cold all winter long. It is possible that you won't get any touch of virus the rest of your life. It is possible that you will get a better job, or a better home, or a better group of friends, or a better this, or a better that. This is totally possible. But the wheels of the human mind start going, "Yes, it is possible, but is it probable?"

That is when the trouble comes. The moment you deal with probability, you have signed away your spiritual birthright. With God all things are possible, and you are a part of God. With God all things are possible, and with you all things are possible. With me all things are possible, but if I deal with the law of probability, I am self-stopped. I have signed away my birthright.

This instruction we call Religious Science arose and has flourished and is meeting the needs of millions of people because enough of us in the early days stayed at the point of possibility and did not speculate on probability. We saw a new church as possible even though it was improbable; otherwise, all we early teachers would have given up. Ernest Holmes and the other early writers would never have written their books. The early Practitioners would never have healed their people if they had not stayed at a level of possibility—"It can be done"—and remained at that level long enough to see it done. There isn't a person in the world in any work who hasn't many a time been tempted to throw his job overboard. You will never know the number of times that I thought I might study how to be a plumber. I didn't, so I am still a clergyman. Times come when you think that you want to get out of the whole thing. Why? Because, all of a sudden, the law of probability takes over your thinking, instead of remembering the spiritual law of possibility.

In your own mind, go back to something that has been bothering you this past week or the past days or the past month, and stop the probability and start the possibility. Stop your probability, because, when you work with the Divine Spirit, all things are possible if you work with the Spirit. Go back to the original idea, and hold to it and stand for it. If the world says that it is improbable, so what! The world has always been wrong anyway. You cannot go by the world thought and the human mind limitations; these are always wrong. The Divine possibility is in every situation.

Where did you get off the beam and forget possibility? It is easy to do this. I have done it, and you have done it. The problem facing you needs you to review it from the level of possibility. If you are sick, it is possible you can be well. If you are in debt, it is possible you can get out of debt. If you are tired, it is possible you can be alert, vital, and energized. At the level of the Mind of God, all is possibility. We have wonderful research in every field of material science, because men spend their lives working on possibility, not on probability. We never would have had the accomplishments we have had in the last 60 years if scientists had not consistently worked on the law of possibility, not on the law of probability. Do the same yourself. You are your own scientist. You are the only scientist you will know. You are your own scientist, just as you are your own dietitian, your own nurse. You are your own everything, because you are the only deciding factor in your own mind. You are the only thinker in your thought experience. You are the only emotion in your emotions.

As the scientist works at the point of possibility, he reaffirms his goal and works toward it. He may be discouraged a thousand times. Every experiment may come out wrong, but he goes right back and re-does it. Whatever his field of research is, when it fails him he does not fail it. He merely goes back and says, "Something is wrong and I am going to do something different because the thing that I want to prove is possible." And he proves it.

Anything is possible even if it isn't probable. Get rid of the probable, and it will be possible. People without knowing it say to themselves, "Why can't a situation change?" It can, but you have to work with the point of "can." Not with "will it," but "it can." When you deal with how to change, you are in the possibility consciousness.

If I work at the level of possibility and hold to it, then I can, and I will, because the world around me has to change as the world within me changes. This is the great law of Mind, that the external is the internal objectified. When I am at a point of divine possibility within myself, I see my world change. But, when I say that in the next year I will probably have so much income, I rest in the negative, and this is all I will get. I have signed away my spiritual independence. I have signed away my initiative. You and I have no way of knowing what the next year is going to produce, except that it will only produce what we produce in it. This is the law of cause and effect, sowing and reaping. The only way I can produce something better than that which has gone before is to know it is possible and to conceive it and become it.

Mentally conceive the possibility of your own perfection. What would you be like if you were perfect? I mean perfect body, perfect wisdom and intelligence, perfectly balanced emotions, because this is the possibility.

The Treatment

This is the eternal recognition. There is a Perfect Cause; therefore, there is a perfect effect. There is a Perfect Mind; therefore, there is a perfect idea. There is a Perfect Love; therefore, there are balanced emotions. I am the possibility of life. Yes, I am the possibility of Life. Amen.

The Sermon

YESTERDAY ENDED last night. The heartaches of the past are the devils of the present, and the creators of evil in the future. If I never say another thing, I have said a great truth. The heartaches of the past are the devils of the present, and the creators of evil in the future. There isn't an individual who at one time or another has not said, "If only I could forget. If only I could forget." You don't want to forget pleasantness. You don't want to forget graciousness, kindness, a love based on a depth relationship. In your anguish you want to forget the problems of the past, the heartaches.

It is well established psychologically that the only thing that really affects us is emotion; we are emotional people, and emotion is the creative power of the mind. This is why balanced religion has always taught the power of love. One of the reasons why the teaching of Jesus caught on so quickly in the Roman Empire was that he was a symbol of love. He was not a symbol of war or hate, as the other gods had been. He was a symbol of love. Being a symbol of love, he interested people much more than did their old gods of hate and of war.

Emotion being the cornerstone of life, then yesterday carries into today only through our emotions, because the memory field is a field of emotional memory. This is why you cannot remember a casual incident that happened ten years ago, but you can remember a heartbreak or some equivalent unpleasantness that shook you up emotionally. Because the remembrance of the evils of the past is a part of the nature of the mind until the mind is cleared through spiritual treatment. Nature arranged this because nature expects its creation to clear its own thought. Man is the creation of God as Mind. You and I have not sought to clear our own minds. We have wanted someone else to do it for us. So, we have devised many ways, many paths, many prayer books, many prayer wheels, many statues, many novenas, many saviors, because we wanted someone else to clear our thought, when, of course, this cannot be done. We have to clear our own thought.

You stand isolated like an island. You are you. You are not the savior, the prophet, or the saint. You are you. I am that which I am, and I can never be less. Therefore, if I am that which I am, then no one can clear my thought but myself; no one can change my belief but my own mind; no one can get rid of the past save my own deliberate  saying to the past, "Begone. Thou art no longer a part of me." Thus, I break the membership of that which I have allowed to remain a member of my corporate mental organization. I have to say to that which emotionally crippled me 10 years, 20 years, 2 years, 3 days ago, I have to say unto these things, "Get thee behind me, Satan: thou art an offense unto me" (Matthew 14:23).

There are two very interesting, simple sentences of Scripture, written by the first Isaiah, who wrote the first third of the Book of Isaiah, at a time when the people were in captivity in Babylon. It was a time of great spiritual progress, even though they were very unhappy living, not as slaves, but living as a foreign element in a distant country, and they wanted to go home. Like most of us, they talked about the past, the good old days, and they kept saying to themselves, "Oh, if only things could be the way they were." They lamented, they wept, and the older generation kept saying, "Oh, if only we could have things as they were." Isaiah speaks up, saying,"Remember ye not the former things, neither consider the things of old. Behold, I will do a new thing; now it shall spring forth; shall ye not know it?" (Isaiah 43:18,19).

What this means is, if your attention is so fixed upon the old patterns, the old habits, the things that used to be, the people that used to be, then you will not even see the new that I make. "Remember not the former things," Isaiah said, "neither consider the things of old." Why? "Behold I will do a new thing and now it shall spring forth; shall ye not know it?"

I know people, and you know people, too, who, no matter what you say to them, will not turn from the past. They view and review the past. They say that it brings them comfort. It does not. It brings them discomfort; that is why they weep. They say that they cannot face the future, which is not so, because they move into the future in every instant. But they view and review the past because it is easier to sit enmeshed in the evils of the past than it is to be creative and progressive about their own future, which is in their own hands. It is easier to weep over that which has been than it is to create that which shall be. Yet, you and I are the people of that which shall be. We are not the people of that which has been.

One of the great advantages of being a part of this Church of Religious Science is that we are not a part of that which has been. We are a part of that which is. It is good that we cannot trace our religious lineage back even a hundred years. It is constructive that we cannot go back, no matter how far, and claim that we are Religious Scientists because of what we were. We are not Religious Scientists because of what we were; we are Religious Scientists because of what we are. That sounds like a paradox, but it is a truth. It is a truth, and we have proven it. It is well that our history of Religious Science is short.

Most religious instruction loses its vitality after the first hundred years. Fortunately for us, we are still in the midst of our most vital era. We are not remembering the things that were before. Religious Science is not going back. It is going ahead. Because, in an unconscious way, we are demonstrating the teaching that "Yesterday ended last night." That an idea concluded is an idea concluded. That an emotional hurt of the past is a concluded concept. And if it is a concluded concept, like Jesus on the cross, we say unto it, "It is finished." Because we are never crucified by the present; we are only crucified by the past.

Each time you weep, each time you hate, and each time that you are angry, you are being operated by the past. Some slight thing at the moment may set you off, but the thing of the instant is not the cause. It is merely the revealing of the pent-up negative emotions in your subconscious mind that have been awaiting a means of release. They have been waiting until you would some day at some instant let down the guard of your own self-decency and allow them to put forth in a stream of uncontrollable feeling. And pour forth they do. I have seen so many weep, not because of what was now taking place, but because of the past. I have seen many in anger, not because of a present hurt, but because of what it evoked out of the past. The door of the subconscious mind opened wide because of an irrelevant idea at the instant that opened the flood gates of the past and allowed the past to flow through.

If the past in its negative emotional states is the damaging action that I have described it as being, then how can you release it? How can you be free of it? You can free yourself of anything when you see the ridiculousness of it. I mean this. We do not have enough self-laughter. We laugh at other people. The radio, television, movie, and theater field pay millions of dollars a year to people to make you laugh, but you are always laughing at an event, a situation, or an individual contrived outside of you to make you laugh. In other words, a comedian on stage falls flat, and you laugh, but when you slip on the ice and fall flat, you don't laugh; you cry. Let a Jackie Gleason fall down and you laugh, but when you fall  down, your tendency is to weep. You laugh at his shame, but you cannot laugh at your own.

The past holds power as long as you feel that the past is greater than the present. As long as you nourish the past so as not to have to compete with the present, then the past has you enthralled. The way to be rid of the past is to see it as experience and growth and nothing else. But, we are so enmeshed in the personalities of the past, the situations of the past, that we slip from the present into the past, and we become past people working in the present.

The present is only explored, the present is only exploited, and the present is only truly known by the people of the future. It is for those people whose thinking is geared ahead, not those whose thinking goes backward. If you like today, then you are willing to release yesterday. If you do not like today, then you had better change your today so that you do like it. If the kingdom of God is on earth as Jesus stated, if we exist in the omnipresence of Mind, Intelligence, Law, and Order, then there is always something you can do about today to make today worthy of tomorrow, and not a repetition of yesterday. It is the repetition of yesterday that prevents the today from becoming the tomorrow.

You have friends who never know the glory of this day, and they will never know the glory of the days to come, because they are too busy with the past. If these same people worked at the business level in the same way, they would be fired by their employers very shortly. No business corporation builds the future on the past. The people who run around telling how the office used to be run ten years ago, are soon replaced. In your office, no one wants to hear about how it used to be and, if the employer finds out that someone is telling about how it used to be when the other man was here, he soon gets rid of you. And, he should! In order to keep business under a law of expansion, it must deal with the future, with that which is not yet created and that which has not yet been sold, but shall be created and shall be sold.

Become intrigued with what you can be, and forget what you were. But, the human mind comes to the fore and says, "How can I be what I want to be?" It names all the material reasons, which are all material lies, because they are not so. Material thinking has never yet created a genius. It has created intellect but not genius. If conditions and environment and all the rest are that important, Abraham Lincoln would have never left Illinois; he would have stayed there. President Wilson would have remained in New Jersey, a very comfortable university president. I would have remained in Rochester, New York, where I was born and raised, and you, whoever you are, would have remained wherever you should have remained, but, thank God we didn't, for we would not have come together at this moment, in this church, if we had.

The people of today are the people of tomorrow, and not the people of the past. When we understand that, we can say, "All the emotional impact of the past is in my subconscious mind. I now declare into my own subconscious mind that negative old memories shall control me no more. They shall not again dictate to me. I shall dictate to them." I say to myself, "All the angers, all the hurts, all the self-pity, all the mourning, all the sorrow, and all the death are no more. They hold me entrenched no longer. I am the Lord, my God. I am not the God of the past; I am the God of the present. No wonder Jesus said, "Let the dead bury their dead" (Matthew 8:22). But those of you who can, follow thou me. Those of you who are able to be a today person in a tomorrow world, follow thou me.

A few followed him. The rest of the crowd remained entrenched in traditionalism, the good old days, the fine old memories, and they became as nothing. The 12 to 18 men and a few women followed him, and these few people, fewer than 30, changed the history of the world. Because something within them allowed them to become today's people in tomorrow's world. They were willing to see the nothingness and the foolishness of the negative hurts of the past. They sensed that here was a Truth of the Living God as a living person, and I mean for themselves. Sensing it, they acted as though it were so, because it was so. So, they wept not over Jerusalem. They wept not over the old kingdom. They wept not over the Temple when it was destroyed. They were too busy going into the highways and the byways, finding people to tell them a great new idea, not an old idea.

That is what this Church of Religious Science does. We are busy going into the highways and the by-ways preaching the good news, for the only good news there is, is new news. Old news isn't good news. Preaching the good news of the individuality of man as the Individuality of God, the personality of man as the Personalness of the Spirit, the freedom of the individual to be in today's world as tomorrow's person, when he is unshackled from the hurts of the past. When it dawns in your consciousness that yesterday ended last night, you are the person that yet shall be in the world that is forever becoming. You consider not the former things of old, because you are letting the Mind and the Heart of God create in you the new thing, and you are ready to create it.

"Remember ye not the former things, neither consider the things of old. Behold, I will do a new thing; now it shall spring forth; shall ye not know it?" Yes, you will know it. Even as I have spoken these words, you have ceased your membership with the hurts of the past. Even as I have discussed this, you have said to the old sorrows, "You are no more." To the old angers, "You have no part in me." To the old resentments and jealousies, you speak unto it as Jesus did when he said, "... for he is a liar, and the father of it" (John 8:44). Seeing that these things no longer have potency, you progress, you advance on all fronts, because now your mind is open to the ideas of God. You are open to that which is forever infiltrating the minds of men with the good news, the new news, the larger concept, the great love.

All of a sudden, you see where formerly you had not seen. You hear that which you have not been hearing. You love where before you had not been loving. All of a sudden, "Yesterday ended last night." All of a sudden, the romance of the Now becomes the intrigue of your emotions. That which is becomes fascinating, and you are so engrossed in the goodness of the tomorrow and the today that you cannot look back except at the good. To look back at the good is always helpful, if you don't look too long. Look back at the good, because the good has been great to all of us. But be ye intrigued with the Now. Be ye fascinated with the present. Speculate on what you are going to be. See yourself as the Divine knows you, the still unexplored, the still not yet fully comprehended, the still greatest phenomena that has ever appeared in evolution.

Tourists are seeking the last little places on this earth where no man has yet trod, or the last little island where as yet there is no Hilton Hotel but there will be. All of this indicates why we have moved our search in matter from Earth to Mars, because we would rather spend billions investigating the outside world than we would spend five minutes contemplating the inside of our own minds.

Within our minds is creation, and here is the only true arena of exploration. We could not put satellites into space if a man hadn't dreamed a dream and thought a thought, planned a plan, and brought forth something new, brought out of the depths of consciousness a new idea. So satellites are up there whirling around in space and will be for as long as I live and longer. They are there because someone in a today's world dreamed a tomorrow's dream. When you explore your own mind with as much interest as you witness the phenomena going on around you, and when you realize that the Creator is not in space or time, but in Mind, and you are in Mind as the creator of your own experience, then you create, not re-create; then you view, not review. Then you see that which is to be seen, not that which has been seen. Then you are worthy of your high calling.

The Closing Treatment

I end our service this morning with a specific spiritual mind treatment, on "Yesterday ended last night." I want you to relax and think with me as I think:

"I believe in God, the living Spirit Almighty. I believe there is One God, One Mind, One Spirit, One Intelligence, One Love. I believe that I individualize the Mind and the Heart of God. Therefore, I now decree into my subconscious mind to remember not the hurts of old. All sorrow, all resentment, all anger, all hate, all that is unlike God in my subconscious mind is now obliterated, destroyed, and shall be remembered no more. Now, I remember the good, and only the good. For my God is now. The Kingdom is come, the Will is done, and Thine is the Kingdom and the Power and the Glory. Amen."

CHAPTER 16

LIMITLESS OPPORTUNITY

Opening Remarks

WE BELIEVE that God is Spirit, and Spirit is Mind. We believe in a governing Intelligence that is forever giving us right ideas, leaving us free to experiment with them. We believe in the power of mind as the Power of God. We believe that every individual is in this Power, has this Power, and uses this Power.

The Psalmist wrote, "He only is my rock and my salvation" (Psalms 62:2); meaning that within us is That which is sound; That which will lead us out of trouble; That which will take us in ways of right action or righteousness; That which will prosper us; That which will heal our bodies; and That which will change our worlds for the better. "He only is my rock and my salvation."

Relax and think of the Mind that has been in every savior and saint, the same Mind that is in you, in me, and in every person, wherever he may be. It is one Mind, common to all men, as Emerson said. It is more than just a human mind. It is a Mind that knows everything, can accomplish everything, wants to do everything, seeks us out in order that It can offer itself to us. It is forever abiding in us, forever thinking through us, forever offering Itself to us. Let us be still and think of the Mind of God, not at a distance, but inside our own thought.

The Treatment

All the Power, all the Presence, all the Life, all the Love, all the Peace and all the Order of God is right now in my mind. It is there because it has always been there. I am now recognizing It and letting this Mind reveal ideas in me. These ideas reveal Right Action. I am now open and receptive to these ideas. They are moving in my mind. They are inspiring me. They are healing old thoughts. They are changing old patterns. They are quickening everything that is good. They are stimulating every right motive, ideal, hope, vision, and glory. The Mind of God is my mind right now. It is great. It is good. It is perfect, eternal, and indestructible. There is One

God, One Mind, One Intelligence. It is mine right here, right now. Amen.

The Sermon

I AM TALKING this morning about "Limitless Opportunity." To put it in a different way, you are free to do anything in the world that you want to do. The Scripture I have selected is, "The world, or life, or death, or things present, or things to come; all are yours" (1 Cor. 3:22).

It is interesting that most people look upon the Bible as a book that tells them what not to do. But this statement of Paul's tells you that you can have what you want; you can become what you want; the Universe is a limitless opportunity for the exploitation by the individual. If you came from one of the older systems of religious thought, you used to be concerned with what not to do rather than with what to do. You were afraid that what you did might cause the Deity to disapprove of you. Therefore, many people remained in a state of lethargy, and they considered this as spiritual. They remained in a state of non-action or repetitive action and considered this to have been virtuous.

This statement of Scripture and many others that I could quote indicate that the people who are near to the heart of God are the people who are active—the people who are adventurous, the people who are able to reach out, to grasp, to give, to share. These are the people who are dear to the heart of God. These people are not merely good; they are good for something. They are projecting, creating, and demanding from life that everything shall be theirs.

If you can be what you want to be and you are not, don't blame this on the Universe; don't blame this on God; don't blame this on religion; don't blame this on the Bible. You can always change. I have been saying this in New York, lo, these 20-some years, and I will be saying it in New York for another 20-some years. You can change. I can change. I can change my thought, which is the place where I have to start. I can create, change, modify, and expand. I can progress or I can retrogress. I can go backwards. I can adjust in the circle of the past and the monotony of the moment. I can live in a dull, difficult, hard way, depleting myself, giving my mind nothing new or fresh to work with; or I can be the adventurer of the Spirit.

I believe that God walks tall in every man and in every woman who ventures in faith. Such a person says, "I shall walk through the valley of the shadow of static conditions, and I shall not fear evil. I know that within me is an Intelligence that is never concerned with the negatives of life. Within me is an Intelligence that is concerned solely with the positives of life."

There is this Mind that is God; this Mind that is perfect; this Mind that knows everything and is knowing everything at the point where you are and at the point where I am. It is not something we invoke. It is not something we cause. It is not something we worship. It is something we know. It is something that is, and because It is, we are; and because we are, we can use That which is.

There is a Divine Intelligence in your mind. Because It is in your mind, you can use It. It is there with all the potentials of life, abundance, peace, power, and everything else in It. But we sit back and say that there is nothing we can do, as the problem is too great, or the medical opinion is such, or the stock market is such. All the time, this Mind in us is saying, "I created you in order to act through you." God made man in His image and likeness, and God saw everything that He had made, and it was good. The Infinite is saying, "I created you out of Myself. I created you in order that, by means of you, I should have expression. I created you to think in terms of the large, the great, the grand, the magnificent, the prosperous, the healthy, and the free."

I look back in my own life and realize that I have often allowed the conditioning thought of the world to limit me, inhibit me, and prevent me. I have let it. I have let it present me with the names of the negatives, and I have accepted those names. The world tells me what I am. The world tells me my age. The world tells me my income. The world tells me my type body. The world tells me whether I am healthy or not. The world tells me whether I am financially free or not. The world is forever telling me what it thinks I am, and 90 percent of the time I believe it. It is in those rare moments of spiritual treatment, when I don't believe what the world says, that I make my spiritual demonstrations.

Jesus said, "My kingdom is not of this world: if my kingdom were of this world, then would my servants fight" (John 18:36). He knew that if you are going to live in the material world as the material world conceives itself to be, you have to fight. You have to argue. You have to battle. You have to get to the top on the basis of trickery and wit. This is what the world believes, but this is not the way it really is. This is not what a Jesus, a Buddha, an Isaiah, or a Paul would think. They would say there was a different way. They would say there was a way, right now in the brain of every living soul, offering Itself to every living soul, saying, "Why argue, why battle, why fight, when all you need to do is to know right action."

Having known, your action will follow your knowing. If you are knowing the negative, then the action must follow that knowing, and it will be negative action. Jesus said if you can know the truth, then you are free. When you know that you are the truth, then you are free of that which is not the truth. When you know that you are healthy, you give no thought to disease.

I am extremely healthy. I haven't thought of the possibility of disease in years. It never enters my mind to watch out for this, or that, or something else. I am healthy. I feel healthy. I act healthy. I don't think disease. When I have money in the bank, I don't think lack. When I am visiting with good friends, I do not think sorrow, loneliness, or unhappiness.

Knowing a positive, my actions and reactions are positive. Knowing a negative, my actions and reactions are negative. I can know either. I can believe what the world says, and the world is telling me that, at my present age, I ought to watch out. I am not interested in watching out for evil. I am interested in watching out for that which is the good on my pathway. This good I have put there through my own thought, and it will unfold because of my thought. It will continue to expand if I keep my mind expanding. My point of attention is on the good, and this is where I intend to keep it. I know that hundreds of you join me in this same idea. When you know a great idea, you experience it as action and reaction.

"This is life eternal, that they might know thee the only true God" (John 17:3). Know that the God in you is indestructible; that the Divine Intelligence in you is immutable. It cannot go away, nor can It come. You don't go to the

Lord. You don't come from the Lord. The Lord doesn't enter into you. You have never been out of God. Whatever It is, you have always been in It. You are in It now, and evermore shall be. But God is saying, "Little man, what do you want? If you can conceive it, you can have it."

In the book, *Your Mind Can Heal You*, Dr. Frederick W. Bailes writes, "Whatever the mind can conceive, it can achieve." When I walk out on the stage of Town Hall, I know that I am going to talk. I know that I shall not falter nor fail. I know it. I have been doing this so long that I know it absolutely. The same thing is true in any area where you excel. Here is an area where you know. Because you know, you act with authority.

It was said of Jesus, "Never man spake like this man" (John 7:46). He spoke from an inner knowing. He knew that he was one with the action of the Universal Mind. He said so. He didn't call it Mind; he called it Father. He said he was one with It; that he was the action of it; and that anyone who looked at him could see It. It is no wonder that they said that no man spake as this man spake. Here was a man who knew and could speak as knowing and, therefore, could convey his conviction to his audience that he did know.

When I go into the barber shop, I believe that the barber knows how to cut hair. If he doesn't, I never go back. I go in the shop and sit down with absolute confidence. Here is a man who knows his business. I don't know how to cut hair. I don't need to know. I have the money to have him do it. He knows what he is doing, but he can't speak in Town Hall on Sunday morning to you here at the First Church of Religious Science. He doesn't know how to do that.

Everyone in Town Hall today and all the radio listeners know what you know in some area, and you act with authority in that area. It may be nothing more than knowing how to scramble eggs. It can be as simple as that. There is a point in your life where you know. Take it and expand it.

Religious Science teaches the law of subconscious mind acceptance. We say that there is One Universal Intelligence or Mind that acts through One Universal Law of Its own action. The Intelligence does the knowing; the Law does the producing. What is known clearly in mind becomes evident through the Law of Mind.

You can walk into a businessman's office and know instantly whether he knows his business. You can walk into a woman's home and know whether she is a good housekeeper or not. You get the feeling about what the person is knowing about himself.

Ask yourself, "What is it that I know, and know so definitely that I act as if I were it, because I know that I am it?" Every idea in your mind is what you really are. That is why we say you are consciousness, meaning you are awareness. You are mind and emotional action and reaction. You are ideas moving in mind. You are acting through a physical body, of course. You are living in a material world—yes. But you are the thinker, and your world is the result of your thought. You are the knower, and your experience is the result of your knowing.

We have a limitless opportunity. Paul said that all things are yours. You may say that it was all right for Paul to say this, but you don't have what you want. You make a list of what you don't have, and each time you make a list of what you don't have, you expand the list. Each time you go through the repetition of everything wrong with you, something gets worse. It has to. When your attention is on the list of what is wrong, naturally there has to be more wrong. You can have all you want, so you can have more trouble. Paul didn't write that his idea was only on the positive side. When your line of attention is on what you don't have, you increase what you don't have. When your point of attention is on what you have, then that expands.

In the book, *The Dynamic Laws of Healing*, the author, Catherine Ponder, writes of a woman who had an unusual physical healing. The person with whom she counseled, after reciting her pains, aches, and problems, was told, "Rest your hand and wrist on the desk in front of you.

Look at it, and find something about it that is right. You spent 20 minutes telling me what is wrong with it; now tell me one thing that is right about your hand and wrist." The woman said, "Well, my little finger is still unaffected." The counselor said, "Rephrase that and make it positive." The woman answered, "My little finger is perfect." The counselor said, "Good. I want you to say a minimum of 200 times a day, "My little finger is perfect, thank God." The woman replied that this idea was ridiculous. The teacher retorted in kind, saying that most spiritual ideas sound ridiculous. Then, the woman said that she didn't know what was spiritual about her little finger. The teacher replied that everything in the Universe is spiritual, including her little finger. Since she should find something to praise and, in her case, she had a perfect finger, she should go home and praise it. The woman praised it and soon became better, and as she continued to praise the hand, the wrist, and the arm, eventually her problems left her.

It is a simple illustration. I assume it is true because the book was written by a person of integrity. Her point was that your attention has to go to something creative in order to get a further flow of creativeness. Your attention has to go to a point that is good in order to have an expansion of good. As long as this woman was contemplating her negative physical condition, she was contemplating things she didn't want, so they became worse. Things do get worse when you contemplate what you don't want. This is the law of life-sowing and reaping, cause and effect. The teacher shifted the woman's attention to a seemingly unimportant factor, but it started the woman finding something that was right.

I often say to people who come to my office to tell me their troubles and seek my help, "What is right with you?" I will hear all about their problems. I know that. I start them off with a constructive, positive note: "What is right with you?" Often, they answer that they do not know because they are so troubled. I can't switch their consciousness from the contemplation of what is wrong to the contemplation of what is right unless something right is determined. There has to be determined at least one point of being right in order to heal any situation. Then the mind can shift.

The whole Universe is waiting for you to decide on a creative good and act upon your decision. All the Intelligence, all the Power, and all the Presence there is, is waiting—waiting for the individual to become the adventurer, waiting for the person to stand tall and say, "I want this, and I shall have this because I see myself as having it. I know myself as possessing it. I claim it. I perceive myself in a situation where it exists. I let this Mind in me, with its Intelligence, its know-how, its infinite abilities, reveal every step of the pathway. It does so in perfect order and right sequence. I let the idea happen because I now have decided that the idea shall happen."

When I have decided that it has already happened, the future is now. Unless I know that I have it in the *now*, I will never have it in the *then*. Only that which I know to be true in the now can appear in my world in the next year. In my own mind I have been doing some thinking, and there are several things that I know are already finished. They are mine. They are in my experience. They as just as clear to me as is the pulpit in front of me or the microphone before me, or the carpet under my feet, or the congregation in front of me in Town Hall. I am certain of them. Under the material law of time and space, they haven't even started to happen, but they will. They will happen because I know they will happen. I not only know they will happen, I know they have happened.

Jesus said, "What things soever ye desire, when ye pray, believe that ye receive them, and ye shall have them" (Mark 11:24). That is the technique of Religious Science. That is the Law of Mind's way of working. I put my attention on the fact that a thing is done, and then the Law of the Spirit does it. "What things soever ye desire, when ye pray, believe that ye receive them, and ye shall have them." You don't get them, and ye shall have them." You don't get them until you believe that you have them. You don't get them by importuning a God. You don't get them by invoking a Deity. You don't get them by good works. You get them through clear, correct knowing.

So many people say that they give to the poor. This is a waste of time. The poor are going to stay poor. They want to be poor. They like being poor, and they are going to stay that way. The Law of Mind says that the rich get richer and the poor get poorer. Each of them is expecting his experience; each of them is knowing it; and each of them is demonstrating.

The principle of limitless opportunity depends on your consciousness knowing; not on a hope, a dream, or a fantasy, but on a clear concept. When it is known, it will be experienced. What mind can perceive, mind can achieve. This is the unconscious method every successful person has used to attain his success. He has known something, and because he has known something, he has experienced something.

I am not discussing intellectual knowing. I am dealing with what I call pure knowing, which is you knowing for yourself and liking what you are knowing. Don't pick a goal that someone else wants you to pick. Choose your own goal. Don't select a goal because it would please your mother. Do it because it would please you. If what you are doing to please your mother doesn't please you, don't do it. Do something that pleases you. You are the only person you are going to live with for the rest of eternity. You may just as well accept yourself, agree with yourself, change yourself, and do what you want. I am sure that what you want to become will be within the framework of good moral character.

To live greatly takes an adventurous spirit. Here is Christopher Columbus sailing out to sea, and all the other great men and women of history that you may name. These people stood up, walked tall, and said, "This I shall do." The world advised them against it. These individuals knew that they could. They knew that it was so, and it became so. Mr. Holmes, in the *Science of Mind* textbook, quotes an old adage, "Act as though it were so, and it becomes so." When you act as though it were so, you are dealing with pure knowing. You are knowing something to be so. When you know that it is so, it becomes so because the law of the subconscious mind makes it so.

We are in a limitless Universe. This country is the most prosperous nation on the face of the globe. We are in the greatest affluence there has ever been in history. We are in an abundant God, an abundant Mind Action, and a Universe that is fantastic in possibility. Yet so many people wander around concentrating on their lists of what they don't have. Watch people, and you will see a list of the "have-nots" written on their faces. They don't have enough of this or that. I am not speaking of money. There are more people desperate for love than there are people desperate for money. It shows on their faces. People are desperate for affection, for warmth, for color, for vitality. There are millions of people in this city now, with everything that this city has to offer, who will sit home alone this afternoon. They haven't anything to do, they haven't anywhere to go. There is no one with whom to go. They are unhappy and miserable. What does the Law of Mind do for these people? It says, "You are unhappy, and you will probably stay that way. You will stay that way until you change what you are knowing."

A person may ask, "How can I change what I am knowing when these are the facts?" If you are going to practice spiritual instruction, you throw most facts out the window. Facts are only evidence of that which has happened. They are not facts dealing with the future. Facts deal with the past. The person may say, "I am so many years old, and this is all the money that I have. These are facts, Dr. Barker." Sure, they are facts. Keep on repeating them, and you are going to get more limited facts just like them. If you are going to deal with facts, then you have to take the limitation that goes with facts.

This church recently had to secure a large mortgage to buy our new church building and the "fact" world told us we could not get it. Every major bank and insurance company in the area said we could not get a mortgage because of "tight money" in the present market. But we got the mortgage because we didn't listen to the fact world. If we had believed in facts, we would still be looking for one. The world of fact said that there was no mortgage available at the present time, and to wait three months. We didn't wait. We knew, and it happened. We didn't go by the world of fact.

When you tell me that your present age is a fact, it is not so—you are nine months older. I have seen people never get much out of life because they believed the facts of limitations as being true. If you are going to believe the fact world, then you might just as well go along with the fact world.

A genius like a Jesus didn't believe the fact world. The great men of science don't believe and accept the finalities of facts. The creative minds of medicine do not believe the fact world. They are spending hundreds of millions of dollars to find the cause of cancer. Why? Because the medical man knows there is a cause that can be found and a cure that can be established. These millions of dollars are not spent on something that will never happen. This research is being done because they know that cancer can be cured, and they are going to find out how to do it. In the meantime, we have the reversal fact thought at the human mind level that it is incurable. The top minds are saying, "There is a cure. Let us work until we get it. We found the answer to diabetes. We found the answer to polio." They believed that they would find these. They are doing cancer research because they believe there is an answer. Some generation—we trust that it will be the present one—will be the fortunate recipients of their findings. These people are not wasting millions of dollars. They are working on a knowing.

When you know the negative, that is what you will be getting. But you can shift your point of attention. The individual can always change his thought. A changed mind will produce a changed condition. The decision is yours. If you are limited, unhappy, or sick, you have built your fortress of belief. You are at peace with it in your own mind. You have analyzed your trouble, and you have your excuses ready. If someone says to you, "You know that you can change your life if you want to," the answer is, "Don't give me that." They want what they have. They have adjusted to it. The only spiritual crime there is, is to adjust to evil. The only sin there is, is to adjust to evil. It is easier to adjust to evil than it is to create good. The man and woman made in the image and likeness of God are creators, not adjusters. These persons are producers, not projectors, not those who adjust and accept.

People say to me, "Dr. Barker, if you were in my situation, what would you do?" I always warn them first. I say, "Do you really want to know?" They say yes, and I tell them. Then they answer, "Oh, I couldn't do that." I may say to them, "You need to get 3,000 miles away from your nearest relative. Go. San Francisco is a lovely city, and all the cities in between. Go." They reply that they can't, so I say, "Then stay here and keep your arthritis." I have learned not to give advice. Everyone asks for it and then resents it.

If you know the truth, you are free from the untruth. Know what you want, and believe that you have it; then you have ceased knowing that you don't have it. Act as though it were so, and it becomes so. The Law of Life is sowing and reaping. This Law is as old as the hills and as fresh as this moment.

The Universe is yours. You can sit back and wait; it lets you do so. Or you can become the adventurer, the thinker, the knower, the actor. You can become the man or the woman whom God created—the person who knows what he wants, acts as though it were so, and it becomes so.

Closing Remarks

There is One Universal Intelligence, Mind, and Spirit—God. It is in us, through us, in action by means of us. It knows what to do and offers this knowing to us. We realize that we live in an unconditioned experience that is conditioned only by ourselves as we function in it. We can always change our experience. Whatsoever things you desire, believe that you have them, the Great Man said, and you will have them. "The world, or life, or death, or things present, or things to come; all are yours" (1 Cor. 3:22).

CHAPTER 17

WHAT ARE YOU WAITING FOR?

THE AVERAGE THINKER accepts the belief in delay as perfectly natural and never questions whether it is actually necessary or not. Such people say to themselves and others that, after all, you can't always have what you want at the time you want it. They are content in this false principle of ineffective living. So, they endorse religions that promise them that they will have their good after death. This lulls them into temporary contentment.

New Thought refutes every statement made above. We know that none of this is true, necessary, or spiritual in origin. We believe in the instantaneous action of the One Mind, God in the consciousness of every individual, for every individual individualizes the total thinking-feeling nature of the causative Mind. All Mind indwells and acts in each person's consciousness. This Mind does not know delay. It does not wait for a right time or for right circumstances. It acts with a right idea fully empowered to demonstrate itself when consciousness decides to have It act.

Time is an orderly arrangement for all of us in which to act and to be in right places at right times. It is not an impediment to effective living. It need not be feared or lamented. It is a framework and not a hazard. Many people resist time. For them it makes a great alibi for their delay-and-wait thinking, which in turn produces delay-and-wait results in their everyday living.

The Universe is an on-time system. It is not concerned with past events, nor is it concerned with future events. God is now; not has been nor will be. This eternal Mind awaits your clear thinking in present terms. Then It can bring to pass what you have decided to have happen. But the whole burden of spiritual demonstration rests on your shoulders. As a spiritual being, you are the deciding factor in the creation of the good you want.

Are you an on-time person? If you are, all life rejoices. All Mind can function in your ready consciousness. There is no delay in your demonstrations. You are an annoyance to those who are always late. Such people cannot understand on-time individuals, nor do they want to understand. Their alibis for always being tardy and delaying their own good keep them from facing the real facts of life, which is consciousness and the way it works. This they do not want to consider.

The Law of Mind will create what you want when you want it, if you will think in on-time ways and be definite in such thinking. The Law of Mind is unaware of hopes, wishes, and past thinking. The Law of Mind is a now creator. Being an affirmative Law, it cannot respond to negative patterns or negative desires. It produces results when a thinker thinks with honesty and definiteness in terms of his demonstration as already made. Ernest Holmes has written that "The Law responds by corresponding."

It may well be that you don't subconsciously really want what your conscious mind thinks it wants. Do you want it because others tell you you should have it? Or, will it please someone important in your life if you have it? Many students of Truth delude themselves; therefore, this New Thought doesn't work for them because they are trying to manipulate rather than create from their own inner sources. The Divine Order cannot respond to manipulation, whimsy, or caprice. It only responds to the sincere student who really uses its principles.

Never seek to demonstrate what others think you should have or do. You are a divinely centered individual with the great spiritual faculty of volition. You have a right to choose for yourself but not for anyone else in this world. To choose correctly for yourself is a great spiritual responsibility. It is much more than merely knowing right from wrong. It entails the serious question of why do I want this that I have chosen? Do I honestly believe that Life will approve? If the answer to yourself is yes, then stop waiting and start the affirmative action of correct on-time thinking in your consciousness.

Your consciousness alone decides what you can have and when you can have it. A real student of divine metaphysics does not let others do his selecting, nor does he blame his wrong selection on world conditions or the times in which he lives. He knows what he wants. He decides to have it. Then all the good there is allies with his thinking to make it happen. This is the correct spiritual method of demonstration. It is the right use of the Creative Process. It is the right use of Thought and Emotion, the two great keys to effective living.

In the consciousness of this writer, unnecessary delay is a metaphysical sin. It is a mistake and carries with it definite negative consequences. It usually indicates a defeated consciousness that is afraid to act on time. It also could be an unconscious fear of the immediate future. It is a means of getting more time in which to think about both sides of the question. This is unhealthy thinking, which can only lead to a stalemate. This is not only a waste of time; it is spiritually erroneous. The sins of omission and commission in consciousness are many. Take a mental inventory, and see yourself as you really are.

No one likes to admit his or her mistakes. They have to be faced and known. They do not need to be discussed with others, nor should they be amplified to cause guilt. To delay is not a serious fault, but one that nags the individual who has the pattern of very often not being on time. This is an annoyance that no one needs and from which no one gains. Spiritual mind treatment will erase it and establish on-time thinking, which is order. Out of this order comes good.

The Universe is constant action. It could never be delayed action. It is now action, and alert minds sense this and follow this guideline to whole living. We believe that the Divine Mind, the Cause of all being, is the harmonious action that benefits all who flow with it and use it. This action never slows down nor does it speed up. It is a divine constant of order. All this is in every person's consciousness at every instant of time. The right action is what you really are. You are consciousness creating and directing causative action.

"I don't know what to do, and that is why I can't decide." This cry comes from the hearts of the always-delay people. Indecision is an unconscious decision to fail.

It is a fear of handling life and meeting its challenges head-on. The world has never been improved by indecisive people. Your individual world will not improve until you decide that it will and act upon that decision. On-time thinkers have no fear of making mistakes. They know that mistakes can always be clarified in ways in which good will still take place. Usually, mistakes are guidelines to new opportunities.

The delay people miss so much of the greatness of being alive in these interesting times. The Universe is waiting for on-time-thinking people to enjoy it to the fullest. Being a spiritual system, it cannot withhold its possibilities from the consciousness of alert minds whose thinking is today's thinking. But, the delay-conscious people cannot know these possibilities or have the blessings that attend them. Such people are too busy with "Shall I or shan't I? What would happen if I did decide?" Missed opportunities are tragic. All the ideas of the Infinite Mind are ours right now, but we have to accept them and act upon them.

The transcendant power we call Divine Love wants each person to have health, wealth, love, and self-expression. It has placed the complete patterns for these four universal essentials in your consciousness. There they will remain latent until known, believed in, and thought about as being the Truth of your consciousness. They are the truth. They always have been the Truth. They always will be the Truth. Whether they are accepted by your consciousness or not, they remain the inviolate Truth. New Thought students do accept them as their premise of being.

Health is based on healthy-mindedness, a spiritually aware consciousness in which affirmative attitudes about life predominate. It is already yours. If you need health in any way, what are you waiting for? Deny the appearance of illness, and affirm that for you it cannot and does not exist. Be definite and clear on this point. Be repetitive until the false condition has gone. Do the same if you have difficulties in your prosperity area, or your personal relationships area, or your job and career area. All of these respond to correct spiritual knowing, and you are the knower who can have the good you want when you decide to do the knowing. Stop waiting and clarify consciousness. You can do it.

CHAPTER 18

THE DEATH OF EVIL

THE LAW OF GIVING is immutable and eternal. You have to give in order to receive. Every New Thought minister has preached this doctrine a hundred times, usually in order to raise funds for a church project. But that is merely a surface concept of a much deeper truth.

Jesus said, "Come, ye blessed of my Father, inherit the kingdom prepared for you from the foundation of the world." An inheritance follows death; it may be the death of a loved one, a distant relative, or a friend, but death is involved. To receive the divine inheritance planned for you from the foundation of the world, you must die to something, or something in you must die. The whole spiritual concept has nothing to do with physical death. It is a death, in the mind, of that which has outlived its usefulness.

We hold on to that which should pass away. We keep old papers, old letters, old photographs, old ideas, old biases. We clasp to our bosoms that which has been, and wonder why the new does not appear. Often we have treated and prayed for weeks that the new shall take place, but have forgotten that we must die to the old before the new can appear. God does not clutter up our lives. We do the cluttering. We fasten firmly to us those things that must pass away, and we thereby prevent the Mind, which makes all things new, from bringing to pass our new desires.

Paul wrote, "I die daily." This man knew the truth of the law of circulation. Old ideas must pass away before new conditions can be born. To inherit what God has planned for you requires your death sentence on that which has completed its course. To deny an idea is to cause its death. Denying it robs it of the nourishment of your thought, and necessitates its withering to nothingness.

You are blessed of the Father, for you individualize the Infinite in order that the Infinite can act at the level of the finite. God forever rests in benediction upon man. Mind expects its individualization to act as God acts. Knowing no evil, it cannot know when man holds on to that which has passed away and thereby fixes the old in the current of the new, damming the streams of consciousness. God forever beholds the immaculate man whom you are. Knowing you as that, the Infinite knows you as the inheritor of all the kingdom of good, the kingdom of perfection.

Your good has been planned by the divine wisdom from the beginning of the world. The cosmic God, thinking cosmically, prepared the good which is yours. Had your thinking not interfered, this good would be yours right now. In spirit and in truth, it is yours right now. It awaits your clearing of the channels of consciousness in order to manifest. So, declare the death of all evil—the evil of your holding on to that which has finished its purpose and that can no longer kindle the flame of desire. Let it be gone, that your inheritance can be born into your world.

The death of evil is the awareness of God. Then the kingdom prepared for you by the divine Knower is revealed. The unconditioned good appears as you cease the conditioning of your thinking. "This one thing I do, forgetting those things that are behind, and reaching forth unto those things that are before, I press toward the mark for the prize of the high calling of God." The man who wrote this had been a rich man in Tarsus. He had been highly educated and greatly respected. Yet he realized that the past was past. He was open-minded to that inheritance incorruptible that had been planned for him from the foundations of the world. He could not afford the luxury of the past re-thinking. He knew God as the new, the creative, and the refreshing.

The new comes only with the passing of the old. The Book of Revelation states that there will be "a new heaven and a new earth," for the old heaven and the old earth shall pass away. What you desire is to you a new idea and a new experience, and it necessitates the death of the old idea and the old experience. Spring appears because autumn has taken place. The old leaves make way for the new; they fall off the tree because the tree cannot hold on to them. But man can hold on to that which should go, and he thereby prevents the appearance of that which should come.

The Father has prepared your inheritance of great, fresh, new ideas and experiences. Blessed is the individual who can make way for the action of God to take place. His mental pathway is cleared of the debris of the past, and the "King of glory"—the new man or woman in the new experience—is able to proceed into the glory of that which has been planned from the beginning of the world. You are the "King of glory" when you have deleted the impediment of that which is no more and have accepted the fullness of that which yet shall be, for always it has been.

CHAPTER 19

A MENTAL VACATION

WE ALL NEED a vacation from our bad habits, and now is a good a time to take it as any. It is inexpensive, requires no new clothes, and the new mental vistas that result from it are glorious. Most people put off this vacation too long, and, as a result, we have formed habits of worry, always talking about sickness and lack, and usually much too much gossip. A few weeks of relief from all that mental negation will do us a world of good.

The mind of the average person—and you and I are average people—is busy with worry ideas the greater part of the time. Almost all the things about which we fret and misdirect our mental possibilities are unnecessary and never happen anyway. We don't like to talk with people who pour out their troubles upon us, and perhaps there are many who avoid us for the same reason.

By talking of good and by concentrating upon ideas of health, joy, peace, and prosperity, we dissolve the old worry states out of our minds; we give ourselves a greater and finer mental vacation than we could ever have if we spent thousands of dollars and traveled hundreds of miles. This new mental vacation can be taken in our kitchen, office, penthouse, or backyard; and it pays rich dividends in peace and prosperity.

That great psychological genius, Jesus Christ, realized that the mental habits of the people of Galilee needed changing. They needed a vacation in mind, and this He offered them. They worried over the same essential problems that we worry about; taxes, governmental problems, sickness, and death. They were just as unhappy as a result of all their negative *thinking* on those wrong ideas, as we are. To those anxious minds, He said, "Follow thou me" into a way of *thinking* and living that is sure; into a Truth that never fails; into a Life that is always wonderful, glorious, and eternal in its ever-expanding activity.

New mental habits were the things He sought to give them; new *thoughts* of good, of peace, of health and prosperity. As we watch the way He *thought* and base our own *thinking* on that intelligent basis, we shall have that perpetual mental vacation in the green fields of new and good mental habits. Great shall be the results from that new mentation. Shall we try it?

CHAPTER 20

DISCOVER YOURSELF

YOU AND I often do not think of ourselves correctly. We sometimes think of ourselves in limited, material terms. There is a widespread need to develop a correct sense of self-awareness. This is aptly illustrated by a non-churchgoing mother's reaction when her small son came home from Sunday school and said that all the children had been asked to repeat over and over again, "Wonderful, wonderful me. I am made in the image and likeness of God." The woman, who saw her little boy as flesh and blood, running around and often being annoying, called the minister on the telephone immediately and complained of the terrible teaching. She was further incensed when he told her that, far from being terrible, the instruction was wonderful and correct.

The fact is that you and I are certainly the ultimate of the Creative Process, because we can do things, create things, and become things that no other form of life can do. We are the Creative Mind in action. When we know this, we begin to see that we are wonderful. The individual is the magnificence of the Creative Process.

We begin to dwell on this; we find ourselves in deep mental arguments because our whole reasoning mind, since the beginning of time, has believed the exact opposite. The whole belief of the collective unconscious of the Universe is the opposite of the statement that "I am the magnificence of God." And, therefore, my reasoning mind comes in and says, "It's not so."

We have reached a point of decision. Each individual has to decide for himself what is *really* so and what is *apparently* so. There is a great difference between the two.

Your depth of spiritual potential is really so. You can ignore it, you can deny it, you need never think about it again. It still remains so. You can deal with the apparently so, and the apparently so is saying that what you believe about your potential isn't so. Man was born to die, man was born to suffer, and so on.

First of all, you don't die; you only change environment. Second, you were not born to struggle. You were born to function in life and handle problems, most of which you create. Every once in a while I think of that. Here I am handling problems, most of which I create—not with intent, not with purpose, but unconsciously I have allowed things to happen.

You and I were born to *become*. We were born as consciousness, for the purpose of expanding consciousness, in the course of which our bodies grew tall, in the course of which we were affected by people, situations, education, and all the rest. It had to be. But you and I started as consciousness on a pathway of expansion, and it's always expanding.

Your consciousness is greater than it was a week ago, because you have had seven days of putting things into it. You have had seven days of believing, and it matters not what you believe; it is still expansion of consciousness. This is probably where the word *soul* originated as a term to describe the individual. Man is a living soul, or man is consciousness.

In the Book of Ecclesiastes, Chapter 7, are these words: "God hath made man upright; but they have sought out many inventions." One of the inventions that started as far back as history can be traced is the invention of two separate powers. One is good and one is evil. That there is a power of evil that can operate, and supposedly does operate, is an apparent truth. It comes in very handy because it explains all the negatives of life. The two-power system is one of the inventions man has created.

We say that there is One Mind which is All Power; that all the evil there is, man has created by misusing that power. No gun has ever shot itself off. No bottle of whiskey has ever opened itself. You can go on endlessly with illustrations. Wherever there are negatives, there are individuals involved. One of the many inventions, then, is this *not-so* truth of the two powers.

Another invention is that to get anywhere, you have to fight; you have to tread over others; you have to use devious ways. That's an apparent truth, but it is not so. It is a false conclusion believed by millions and used by millions, but that doesn't make it so. A negative belief is not a truth. It is a false concept of a truth. The truth is that there is One Power, One Presence, One Mind, One Cause, and we are free to use it in any way we want to use it.

Many children actually believe in Santa Claus because their parents say he is so. We often accept a thing as authority without investigating it. So we have accepted ourselves as what? Mortal, average human beings. These are the untruths that you have to be set free from, because you are the magnificence of the Creative Process.

By knowing what you are, you also know what you are not. Then you are not subject to the ills, the problems of the race or the group in which you function.

There used to be a book with the title, *There Is No Need to Be Sick, Unhappy, Miserable, Lonely*. People used to look at it and grab it, because it awakened something intuitively in them. It awakened an unconscious knowledge of what they really were. It stirred something. Maybe just by saying it, it stirs something in you. Does that mean you will never have any of these problems? Probably not. But at least it is a call. It is a call to remember that which is so.

Sometimes you probably have said, "I am unhappy." Then there came times when you were happy again. The unhappiness came, was accepted, dwelt upon, worked to its conclusion, and then something restored the balance. And so you could say, "I am happy."

To us, the happiness is that which is so, and the unhappiness was only that which was apparently so. It was a temporarily accepted non-truth. Because the individual believed in it, he experienced it. But you can always change belief. This is what every spiritual system has been trying to say: You can always change what you believe when you have decided to change it.

Some of the old beliefs that we have held have roots that go down, down, down into the subconscious mind, and they are very hard to uproot. Some of these things that are not so, but appear to be so, have been nurtured for years. When we start by trying to dismiss them, it is not easy. It takes definite, specific work, starting with intention and decision, and followed by a constant watching of the mind.

You were not born just to get through life, nor was I, nor was anyone else. You and I were born to create. There is no other reason for our existence. This is the great drive. It has been given many labels by many authorities. Freud said it was a sex drive. Other people—like us—say it is a divine drive. It matters not the name. We have to fulfill the need. If we want to keep our sanity, we have to express, we have to release, we have to project, because it is our nature to do so.

One of our earlier teachers said that the whole thing could be summed up with a single sentence—that we are Being becoming Being. Or we are consciousness by means of which the Infinite knows itself. We are that by means of which whatever it is, knows that it is.

Here are some statements for you to think about: *I am spiritual. I am creative. I do not fit in all patterns. I am original. I am unique.* The list can go on and on. If you use these statements, they will remove whatever remains in your mind of the idea of man the sinner, man the no-good, man who is going to perdition, and all the rest. Remember that statement made in Ecclesiastes: "God hath made man upright; but they have sought out many inventions." Man has sought out all the inventions to discredit himself, because he couldn't believe what he really was.

Take time to remember that you are creative cause. You are expression. You are a thinker who can think greatly. You are mind and emotions with the capacity not only to think greatly, but to love greatly. Knowing this, you have discovered yourself, so let there be no more self-deprecation, no more poor-little-me, and no more believing that everyone is against you. Put aside the pettiness of past thinking and the stupidity of wrong use of emotions.

You are that which thinks greatly, thereby creating greatly. You are that which feels greatly, thereby giving content to your thinking.

CHAPTER 21

YOUR ETERNAL MARRIAGE

EVERY CUSTOM originated as a symbol, and marriage is the symbol of unity. I want to look at marriage metaphysically, because it is an explanation of the conscious and subconscious mind and their interaction. The conscious mind is the objective symbol, and the subconscious mind is the subjective symbol. The conscious mind inseminates the subconscious mind, which then brings forth its demonstration or result.

Ernest Holmes had a phrase that the only begotten is forever begetting the only begotten; meaning this interaction of the spirit as the objective principle with the soul as the subjective principle, is forever bringing forth the only begotten, which is creation. That's the whole thing, the spiritual marriage, infinite mind, both conscious and subconscious, self-sustaining. The spiritual marriage.

This marriage cannot have divorce, because you can't get rid of either of those two minds. You cannot stop this interaction between your conscious and subconscious mind. As long as you are able to select, by making a decision, the marriage is going on.

Some of the mystics have talked about the eternal marriage. They were talking about the balanced person in a balanced life functioning intelligently. Now, as you know, the conscious mind could put very bad ideas into the subconscious mind, which it will bring forth as a child, or result. But the eternal marriage would be the balanced mind creatively used, bringing forth the only begotten—the world of creation, which would be the kingdom of heaven.

You see, the one has to become the two in order to become the three. That's why it says that God created us after His image.

The elements of the Infinite Mind are seemingly divided to bring forth the third element, which is creation. The Infinite, which is pure individuality and pure personality, became individualized and personalized to bring forth creation. So, your world is the result of your wedding. It has nothing to do with whether you are married to another living soul, because this is the world you have brought forth out of the depth of your own soul. So, since you are the progenitor of your own field of creation, you have the responsibility to select that which is best for your world. Anything you select for your world that adds beauty, joy, love, or happiness is the proper use of the eternal marriage.

When you are not using your eternal marriage correctly, when you have lack, illness, or emotional upheaval, you have created a temporary separation in your marriage. Now, although you cannot have a divorce in your marriage, every time you shatter the balance, you cause a separation, and this separation on the mental level produces disharmony on the physical plane. But, when you regain your balance through correct use of Mind, you become united with yourself, and the marriage works again.

Separation can also be caused by alcohol, drugs, and emotional turmoil. We have all seen people drunk, completely out of balance with themselves and with life. This is a temporary separation of this person's fundamental unity. The conscious mind is unable to select in a balanced way, so the subconscious is not bringing forth creative ideas. When he sobers up, the balance is restored, the conscious and subconscious interact intelligently; and thinking, feeling, and creating are again functioning as a joyous experience.

So it is with drugs, and especially, so it is when we let other people decide for us. When we allow outside things to determine our selection, our creation of our world, we create a separation in our marriage, and bring forth fruits that we do not want, that make us unhappy, that create an internal imbalance.

We've all seen people like this. They believe and act on all they read in the newspapers, on everything they're told, and they live lives of frustration, sickness, and want. They have allowed another factor to determine the quality of their lives. Occasionally, I let this happen in my life, but when it does, I say to myself, "Stop!" I look at myself in the mirror and say, "I am a spiritually perfect individualization of Infinite Mind, using this Mind as me constructively. I am creating my own experience rich in happiness, harmony." That generally gets me back on the track, restores my eternal marriage, and permits me to function again as a creative outlet of the Infinite.

You can do it, too. When you know yourself as a unified function of God, creating out of yourself an orderly and balanced world, you will experience it. Is it easy? Not always. You see, it's so easy to let the other stuff in. So easy to create a separation. But correct mental knowing will pull you through.

Now, let's get back to the mystic. I am my own husband. I am my own wife. I am my own child. I am a unit. I am forever begetting, because I am forever putting something into my subconscious mind. So we arrive at the Law of the Subconscious Mind. The subconscious mind doesn't know what is coming into it, but it knows it has to produce it. So, whatever you put into it will be produced in your life as result. You might not instantly recognize it as a different pattern in your life, but it's there, so select with wisdom. In the infinite variety of the One Mind there is vast potential for every one of us, and when we select our lives creatively, we live in balance. We live with perfect interaction of our conscious and subconscious minds. We are the eternal marriage.

CHAPTER 22

A NEW TEACHING FOR A NEW WORLD

Creating Health, Happiness, and Harmony

AN ESSENTIAL BELIEF of New Thought is that the Universe is an intelligent creation of an intelligent Mind. This Mind is God. Older theologies have proclaimed God as the Creator, but have not always given a logical or intelligent outline of the method by which the Creator becomes the created. The New Thought Movement, with its understanding of God as Mind, explains creation as a logical result of the Divine Mind giving birth to ideas, which take form. This process is an eternal one, for creation is never complete; it is forever going on.

This spiritual process by which the cosmic system has come into being is based upon divine law, a law of mind action. The conditions, limitations, and possibilities of each of us are dependent upon the ideas our consciousness projects into form. We are created in the "image and likeness" of the Universal Mind, and, as Jesus said, have been given all power and all authority to be the Light of our own world.

This indwelling power and authority consists in our ability to grasp the spiritual ideas of the God-mind and to think those ideas into form. We are spiritual beings living in a spiritual Universe governed by spiritual law. If our experience does not seem to bear witness to this fact, it is due to our own misuse of ideas.

Jesus Christ redefined our oneness with Spirit. God is Spirit, and we are made in the image and likeness of the Spirit. Jesus came to inject into our consciousness the idea of our own divinity. He assured the individual that everything the Christ in Jesus of Nazareth accomplished could be accomplished by the Christ of each individual. The indwelling Father to which Jesus referred is the universal Christ Principle in every son and daughter of God. As students of this Truth, we apply our knowledge of our inherent perfection as spiritual beings to human needs and thereby heal the sick, prosper the poor, and bring peace to confused minds.

The healing of body and affairs is the natural result of spiritual Causation operating through the mind of man.

Health, happiness, and prosperity are the inevitable result of our thinking the thoughts of God after Him. A perfect Cause does not produce an imperfect result. As our thought turns to Spirit as the "cause, medium, and effect" in our life; as we recognize our oneness with God and therefore with all of the attributes of God, realizing that nothing unlike Perfection can belong to the Christ of man, we bring forth into our life "the fruits of the Spirit," some of which are happiness, health, and prosperity.

These great benefits, resulting from the immutable Law of God (which is always the Law of Good), are impersonal and omnipresent. They work for one and all. Creed, race, and personality have nothing to do with this immutable law of mind in action.

Heaven and hell are the results of our use of ideas. If we turn to the indwelling Christ Mind and draw our ideas from that Source, we live in heaven here and now. If we turn to the external world and the opinions of others, we build for ourselves a hell here and now. New Thought affirms that we are in heaven here and now and are as spiritual as we ever will become. As we turn from the race beliefs in sin, sickness, lack, and death, to the living ideas of Jesus Christ (which are life eternal, opulence, radiant health, and permanent harmony), we will create for ourselves a wonderful world in which we will live as intelligent spiritual beings.

New Thought is not so much a religion as it is an approach to spiritual Truth. It does not tell us what to do; it tells us who we are, and we, by perceiving our own spiritual nature, automatically begin to change our attitude to mind. With the adjustment of our thought, outer conditions in our life are changed accordingly.

The New Thought Movement is proving, in the life of every sincere student who applies it, the practical results of thinking with the Christ Mind and loving with the Christ Heart.

DR. BARKER'S FOUR BASIC TREATMENTS

I. HEALTH

There is one God, one Mind, one Life, one Vitality, one Energy, one Perfect Functioning of all Ideas in Mind. My Health is the action of an Infinite Intelligence functioning perfectly, functioning normally, functioning in Order, all Ideas working perfectly, completely, and divinely; so that there is neither over-action nor under-action. There is only normal action. There is no principle of straining. There is the principle of ease. Therefore, I am not under the law of tension. I AM under the law of ease, order, harmony, normalcy of all functions. So my consciousness, which is the CAUSE and maintenance of my body, is now circulating its Ideas perfectly. It is now assimilating all ideas perfectly. It is now eliminating all Ideas that have finished their course. It is now working in divine order and on time. This is my health, and I rejoice in it. My subconscious mind accepts this. And so it is.

II. WEALTH

This is a treatment for total freedom in money.

Let us enter into this with joy, because we are dealing with a principle of eternal abundance. This Universe is never poor. The Universe never runs out of leaves for trees. It never runs out of weeds for gardens. The Universe is always abundant, always rich, always productive. Therefore, I, as a part of the eternal system, a part of the eternal process, of the eternal mechanism, I am that same abundance. Any and all limited subconscious patterns regarding money in my subconscious mind are now eliminated, neutralized, and gone. Every concept in my subconscious mind regarding the income and disbursements now expands. I am free in the freedom of money. Money is God in action. Money is God in circulation. Money is Life itself, flowing in, flowing out. Money is good. It is great. I appreciate it. I praise it. I rejoice in it. Money is an idea in the mind of God, of ease and freedom. I AM the Idea in the Mind of God; therefore, these two ideas now come together, coalesce, and become one, are one. I am money. I decree this in my own mind. All right. So it is.

III. LOVE

This is a treatment for communication with people. It is that which unifies, unites, and maintains as free people. It is without possession, without domination, without control.

There is one God, one Mind, one Spirit in an eternal emotional field, a balanced emotional field through which ideas can communicate, one with another. This is LOVE. Therefore, I decree that I AM this great composite idea of the Infinite Mind moving in an arena of balanced emotions, giving and receiving Life, Love, Ideas; all people communicate with me; I communicate with all people. Therefore, there are no closed doors. All channels of communication between myself and any other living soul—these channels are open and they flow both ways. So I love to Love with the Love of God. People Love me with the Love of God. This is balanced, perfect communication. Any and all subconscious impediments to this treatment are now neutralized, nullified. It is definite in my consciousness now, and it will operate now and forever more shall be. So be it.

IV. SELF-EXPRESSION

This treatment is for personal relationships—one of those difficult fields of life. It will do anything that you believe it can do.

The need of the soul to express individuality—which you are. We all have this need. There is one individuality—the eternal I AM that is God. This is oneness with God. This is my individuality right now. This individuality includes the totality of intelligence, love, wisdom, beauty, and truth. It has within it everything necessary for my full self-expression—in all fields that I select, in all avocations as well as vocations. Therefore, I now declare that I have full self-expression. Any and all subconscious conditioning that would limit or obstruct my total self-expression is now denied, neutralized. I AM able to express my full and complete self. I accept this in my subconscious mind.

So be it.

About the Author

The late Dr. Raymond Charles Barker, an important figure in the New Thought Movement and past president of the International New Thought Alliance, was the founder of First Church of Religious Science in New York City and past president of Religious Science International.

We hope you enjoyed this Hay House book.
If you would like to receive a free catalog
featuring additional Hay House
books and products, or if you would
like information about the Hay Foundation,
please write to:

Hay House, Inc.
1154 E. Dominguez St.
P.O. Box 6204
Carson, CA 90749-6204

or call:

(800) 654-5126